Comments on other *Amazing Stories* from readers & reviewers

"You might call them the non-fiction response to Harlequin romances: easy to consume and potentially addictive."
Robert Martin, *The Chronicle Herald*

"Tightly written volumes filled with lots of wit and humour about famous and infamous Canadians."
Eric Shackleton, *The Globe and Mail*

"This is popular history as it should be ... For this price, buy two and give one to a friend."
Terry Cook, a reader from Ottawa, on **Rebel Women**

"Stories are rich in description, and bristle with a clever, stylish realness."
Mark Weber, *Central Alberta Advisor*, on **Ghost Town Stories II**

"The resulting book is one readers will want to share with all the women in their lives."
Lynn Martel, *Rocky Mountain Outlook*, on **Women Explorers**

"[The books are] long on plot and character and short on the sort of technical analysis that can be dreary for all but the most committed academic."
Robert Martin, *The Chronicle Herald*

"A compelling read. Bertin ... has selected only the most intriguing tales, which she narrates with a wealth of detail."
Joyce Glasner, *New Brunswick Reader*, on **Strange Events**

"The heightened sense of drama and intrigue, combined with a good dose of human interest is what sets Amazing Stories *apart."*
Pamela Klaffke, *Calgary Herald*

GHOST TOWN STORIES OF ONTARIO

AMAZING STORIES®

GHOST TOWN
STORIES OF ONTARIO

Maria Da Silva & Andrew Hind

HISTORY

James Lorimer & Company Ltd., Publishers
Toronto

James Lorimer & Company Ltd., Publishers acknowledge the support of the Ontario Arts Council. We acknowledge the support of the Government of Canada through the Book Publishing Industry Development Program (BPIDP) for our publishing activities. We acknowledge the support of the Canada Council for the Arts for our publishing program. We acknowledge the support of the Government of Ontario through the Ontario Media Development Corporation's Ontario Book Initiative.

ONTARIO ARTS COUNCIL
CONSEIL DES ARTS DE L'ONTARIO

Canada Council
for the Arts

Library and Archives Canada Cataloguing in Publication

Hind, Andrew
Ghost town stories of Ontario / Andrew Hind and Maria Da Silva.

(Amazing stories)
ISBN 978-1-55277-412-0

1. Ghost towns—Ontario—History. 2. Ontario—History, Local.
I. Da Silva, Maria II. Title. III. Series: Amazing stories (Toronto, Ont.)

FC3070.G4 H55 2009   971.3   C2009-900648-0

James Lorimer & Company Ltd., Publishers
317 Adelaide Street West, Suite 1002
Toronto, Ontario
M5V 1P9
www.lorimer.ca

Maps by Peggy McCalla

Printed and bound in Canada

Contents

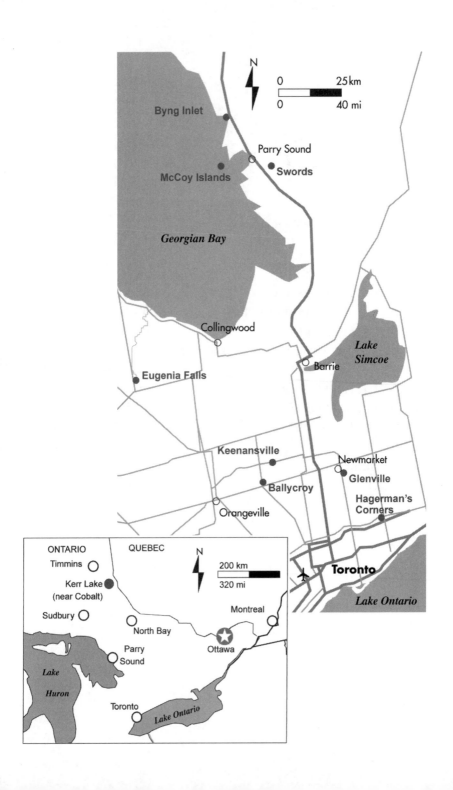

Prologue

J ack Sword's creased face spreads into a smile as he recalls the building in which he had been born 89 years earlier. He had spent the first eights years of his life within the Maple Lake Hotel, running along richly carpeted hallways and playing in the cavernous barroom, oblivious to the fact that his home was once a bustling wilderness resort. Despite the passage of years, Jack maintains vivid memories of the building. He remembers that the barroom had a separate entrance so that well-heeled American tourists wouldn't have to cross paths with "common" lumbermen and farmers. He also calls to mind the large mirrors that hung over the bar, like something straight out of a western. But his strongest memories are of his family, the enterprising pioneers who lent their name to the now-lost hamlet of Swords. Annie Sword, Jack's aunt, had once run the hotel. "Auntie Annie," a very stern woman, was protective of her hardwood floors and fine carpets, so she'd sit on the verandah and thoroughly inspect the boots of anyone entering to ensure that they didn't have caulks (spikes *to provide grip) on their soles. If someone did have caulked boots, she'd ask that they be removed. If the gentleman refused, she'd order him to stomp each boot on a wooden shingle. The shingle would stick to the caulks and then the gentleman would be free to go on in for a drink. Anyone who still refused was barred entry ... and faced the wrath of a strong-willed woman. With no other option for drink and companionship in the area, there were very few individuals who tested Auntie Annie. Jack sits silently for a moment as he savours the story, one of many from the Sword family now relegated to aging memories. Jack's eyes light up, the fire in them rekindled as another tale springs to mind. "And then there was the time ...," he begins. We sit back and listen as Jack Sword regales us with yet another ghost-town tale.*

Introduction
What is a ghost town?

Many people have different definitions of what a ghost town is, and that leads to certain expectations. It's perhaps worth explaining what we consider a ghost town.

Certainly, the truest form of a ghost town is one that conforms to Hollywood imagery and our own imagination: a completely abandoned community, hidden away in some forgotten corner of the world, buildings hauntingly aged but yet still standing. These are the most spectacular ghost towns, but they are also the rarest — especially in locations that are easily accessible.

Our definition, as writers and historians, however, extends beyond this perception. To us, a ghost town is "a community that is merely a shadow — or spectre — of what it once was." It doesn't have to be completely abandoned, but it does have to be wrapped in a ghostly shroud, with the majority of its businesses gone, a population greatly reduced from its heyday, and an intangible sense of abandonment and loss.

With the popularity of rural living, many ghost towns

are seeing some renewed inhabitation. Keenansville, for example, once one of Central Ontario's most completely ghosted villages, has recently seen some modern homes built on former pioneer lots. But what's still missing is the sense of community that once defined Keenansville. These modern-day residents are commuters simply living here for convenience, and since a scattered collection of homes does not make a community, Keenansville remains relegated to the history books, a once vibrant village long gone.

Generally speaking, the farther a ghost town lies from growing cities the more pure it remains. It would be tempting to focus on these more remote communities and their stories, but we opted not to do so for several reasons. First, we realized that by doing so we would be ignoring some fascinating stories. Ballycroy, for instance, a former village whose history is laced with all the requisites of great drama — passion, violence, murder, great success and painful loss — lies less than an hour's drive from Toronto and close to several growing urban centres. We simply couldn't resist an opportunity to tell this community's story, even though it remains home to a handful of souls.

Another reason not to focus solely on the more complete ghost towns is practicality, since most of them lie in the far reaches of Northern Ontario. We want to encourage people to experience history first-hand, to go out and explore the rich heritage that these forgotten communities represent, to gain a tangible appreciation for history that cannot come solely from reading a book. To that end, we decided to include several ghost towns within a comfortable drive of the Greater Toronto Area and the majority of Ontario's population.

We have aimed to bring to life the histories of nine villages within the pages of this book. However, for those willing to make the effort to actually visit one of these vanished communities, history comes alive in a much more intimate manner. As the wind rushes down overgrown roads or swirls around foundation holes it carries echoes of the past, and when you touch a tombstone or a weathered building you can't help but feel the pain and disappointment of those who saw their hopes and dreams dashed by fate.

These tales of disappointment are often sad to hear. Perhaps that's why they are so rarely told; we are a culture that celebrates the winner and casts aside the loser. But if you believe as we do that a community has a soul, then you must also believe that these "ghosts" are restless in death, tormented not so much by their demise but by the callous way in which they've been forgotten. We have taken it upon ourselves to tell their stories, to keep their memories alive, and to pay tribute to these villages and their role in Ontario's development.

Ghostly Ghost Town Stories

Ghost town. The very name conjures up images of weathered buildings with sinister visages, overgrown cemeteries shrouded in fog, wind rustling dried leaves down eerily silent streets — and of course, restless spirits of the dead. The most common question we get after exploring one of Ontario's vanished villages is, "Did you see any ghosts?" It seems unavoidable: in most people's minds, ghostly towns must automatically also include ghostly inhabitants.

This can sometimes be a detriment. After all, when we're trying to tell these communities' stories, it becomes very serious for us, and very personal. Occasionally — thankfully, very occasionally — people get the wrong idea about our work: "You think the village is haunted?" Some take us a little less than seriously, others are offended. We have to then painstakingly explain that ghost towns do not equate to wraiths or revenants, and that the only spirits we're looking for are those that defined the nature of the community in question.

In most cases, the ghost town of the imagination is far removed from that of fact. But not always.

Sometimes, despite what we're actually looking for, we do stumble upon tales of the supernatural. A surprising number of ghost towns do indeed seem to be haunted, or were at one point. We've even had experiences that were unsettling and inexplicable.

These stories were often central to local lore and too engrossing to be left out of this book. When a featured community is haunted by a ghost (or in one case, as many as six), we have included the story at the end of the chapter to which it relates.

Maybe there's a reason after all why the human mind automatically connects ghost towns with ghosts.

Visiting Ghost Towns

There's no doubt that visiting a ghost town can be a fun and rewarding experience. However, we'd like to pass along some hints, garnered in many cases from our own travels and travails, to ensure that things go smoothly for you.

When to Go

Ontario is a large province and conditions may vary greatly by geographic region, but in general the ideal time to visit a ghost town is in early spring or late fall when there is no foliage to obscure hidden remains. Trust us when we assure you how difficult it can be to explore ghost towns in the height of summer. When visiting Swords, we nearly walked past a two-storey home, located not more than 100 feet off the road, because of the dense brush of the regrown forest. And this is the time of year when the clouds of mosquitoes are at their worst.

In early spring or late autumn, the path of old roads can be clearly discerned, foundations located and old buildings enjoyed and photographed. These are also much more atmospheric reasons: the leafless, colourless landscape adds a touch of the macabre that seems to enhance the ghost-town hunting experience.

What to Expect

There is often much to see. Frame buildings are the rarest finds. Many were scavenged for their wood, and they tend not to stand up well to the elements anyhow. Often, such buildings will have been reduced to rotting and sagging shells, their original purposes ill defined. Always proceed with care around these ancient structures — all uninhabited buildings should be considered unsound. Much more frequent than finding entire buildings are relics of former habitation. Foundation holes will provide tell-tale evidence of buildings long gone; fence posts will often denote farmers' fields; and vague trails leading off into regenerated forests will speak of abandoned roadways and railway lines. Watch for lilac bushes — these hardy shrubs are not native to Canada and were brought over by settlers to beautify their properties. The presence of a lilac shrub will almost always betray former human presence. Some relics may be located on private property. While we've found most landowners to be hospitable and willing to grant permission to explore, it's important to always respect private property. Do not trespass. It reflects badly on all of us who enjoy the experience of exploring Ontario's past through her ghost towns. Remember that most ghost towns are located in the wilds. Dress accordingly. Wear sturdy hiking books, as well as both long pants and a long-sleeved shirt to protect against mosquitoes and poison ivy.

Chapter 1
Ballycroy

Location: East of Orangeville, along a gravel road 1 km north of Highway 9 on Highway 50.
Driving Time from Toronto: 1 hour.

The ghost town of Ballycroy has changed greatly since the days when horses struggled to pull heavily laden wagons along its rutted roads and when logs were cut down by the hundreds to feed the insatiable appetite of the local sawmills. Most of the buildings have long since been reclaimed by the forest or ravaged by time, and the once teeming population has been reduced to a mere handful.

The few remnants are shadowed by overgrown brush and trees and are all but forgotten. Yet it feels as if time has stood still here. Ballycroy is a strangely peaceful place, and the echoes of those who lived and died in the village can still be heard amongst the trees, along the empty street and in the foundation holes. They whisper the story of Ballycroy's heady rise and tragic fall.

By 1810 or so, settlers were already spreading outwards

from Toronto into the surrounding counties, pushing the network of roads farther into the wilderness. Settlements rose up along these roads, and when two major roads intersected a village of some importance would appear. This was the case of Ballycroy, which straddled the road north from Toronto and the road east from Orangeville.

The first settler to arrive was Samuel Beatty, who established a sawmill on the nearby Humber River in 1819. This mill was probably the first anywhere in Adjala Township (in the south of Simcoe County), and being the first it helped ignite the local economy. At its peak, the mill's whining blades were cutting 15,000 feet of pine and hemlock annually.

Other settlers began to arrive soon after Beatty established his sawmill, mostly Irish Catholics who named the growing village after a town in their homeland. It was an ideal location for a community. The forests provided lumber aplenty, the soil hereabouts was extremely fertile and the nearby Humber provided power for up to four mills. Perhaps more importantly, businesses in the little hamlet of Ballycroy began to benefit by catering to the traffic that passed along the two busy roads.

There was nearly a tragic reversal of Ballycroy's fortune in 1837 when a rebellion broke out in Ontario. Led by fiery journalist and politician William Lyon Mackenzie, the rebels wanted greater political involvement for the common man and an end to rampant corruption in government. They enjoyed few rights and were considered on the fringe of society, so it is unsurprising that many of those taking up arms were Irish Catholics.

News of the rebellion's outbreak whipped the province into a state of panic, and armed vigilante bands composed of pro-British citizens began springing up to arrest suspected rebel sympathisers. It did not matter if one was politically active or not; anyone of Irish Catholic heritage was automatically held under suspicion. Many Loyalists in Adjala Township began casting a distrustful gaze upon the village of Ballycroy, convinced that its Irish citizens were conspiring to join in the revolt. The fact that Mackenzie had visited the community only months earlier and regaled the populace with a blustery tirade against the government only added fuel to the fires of suspicion.

Tension mounted. Not willing to wait helplessly for the traitors of Ballycroy to reveal themselves, several dozen British farmers decided to strike a pre-emptive blow. In a frenzy of fear and paranoia, these otherwise God-fearing and law-abiding citizens were prepared to butcher the entire male population of the little farming community.

Darkness had descended upon the sleeping village. Men, women and children huddled under blankets as cold winds whistled through the trees outside. They were blissfully unaware of the danger approaching.

Outside, shadowy figures darted from tree to tree, their stealthy approach masked by the natural sounds of the night. Those few who heard noises outside their homes chalked them up to the rustling of dead leaves, branches scraping against buildings, the hooting of owls or the scurrying of wildlife. They rolled over and went back to sleep, never imagining for a second that men armed with hatchets and guns — men intent on murder — were stalking their quiet streets.

Weapons were readied and the assault was about to begin when suddenly a rider mounted on a lathered horse arrived bearing word of Mackenzie's defeat at the Battle of Montgomery's Tavern. With the apparent threat of rebellion now gone, the mob dispersed without firing a shot. The villagers of Ballycroy, who in fact remained loyal to the Crown throughout the rebellion, had no idea how close they came to disaster that night.

Fate continued to smile on the community for a time. Ballycroy gained a post office of its own in 1856, always the first sign that a community had come of age. When the town was at its peak in the 1860s, other important buildings included a chapter house of the Loyal Orange Order, two blacksmiths, a woollen mill with an annual production of $200, a hat factory, two stores, a harness maker and three hotels. Beatty was still running his sawmill, and had added a shingle mill and a flourmill to the mix. By now, however, he faced stiff competition from the flourmill of James Thurston, and sawmills operated by George Hannan and William Brawley. Francis Brawley, William's brother, ran a distillery, which provided a ready supply of spirits for the village hotels.

It was these hotels that gave Ballycroy its well-deserved

reputation for rowdiness. With whiskey costing a mere 12 cents a gallon, alcohol flowed liberally in the barrooms. They tended to be boisterous, and booze-fuelled donnybrooks — for which the Irish were famous.

Generally, the brawling sides were decided along religious lines — Protestant versus Catholic. James Feheley, an Irish hotel proprietor, was considered the leader of the village's Catholic thugs. A man with a hair-trigger temper and devil-may-care attitude, he and his group of roughs would attack any lone Protestant travelling along the roads after dark. Of course, the Protestants of nearby communities would occasionally strike back. Captain Wolfe of Palgrave, an old soldier in the British Army, could not let these slights go unanswered. He and his comrades would ride to Feheley's hotel to settle the score.

> *There, after backing his mount up against the bar-room door, he would dig in his spurs and the charger would oblige by kicking in the door. Needless to say, a scrap began at once and was waged until either side called 'enough,' or until the Orangemen, confronted by an overwhelming number of Ballycroy reinforcements, struck for home.*

Feheley didn't just direct his hatred towards travellers. He seemed to reserve his greatest disdain for James Small, the owner of the community's Protestant hotel. While religious tensions definitely ran deep in Ballycroy, the root of Feheley's animosity was undoubtedly business related. Simply put, he was envious of his competitor's success.

James Small was a real entrepreneur, a man of many parts who grew wealthy in the thriving village. He owned a store and operated the post office, and his hotel was easily the most prosperous in Ballycroy. It was frequented by stage-coaches that dispensed patrons, many of them well-to-do, literally onto its front steps, and Small routinely hosted lavish parties for his guests. The highlight of the social season was the Ballycroy January Ball, which was attended by well-heeled people from as far away as Toronto.

While a lid was kept on the simmering tension between Feheley and Small for a time, it finally boiled over in dramatic fashion in 1875. Sadly, innocent people paid the highest price. The still, dark night of April 29 was suddenly interrupted by calls of alarm, and the blackness pierced by bright red flames. James Small's Hotel was alight, the flames hungrily licking at its walls and climbing rapidly towards the roof. Villagers rushed to fight the inferno, but by the time they arrived there was precious little hope of saving the building. Flames could be seen racing through the halls and engulfing entire rooms in mere minutes.

That's when the villagers saw them — three young women who were employed in the hat factory, framed by the orange glow of flames. They were struggling desperately to open their second-storey window and reach safety. Faces

Ballycroy headstone for three milliners who tragically burned to death.

streaked with tears and twisted by fright, they died horribly as the fire embraced their bodies. The sight of the women dying before their very eyes was a sight few in Ballycroy would ever forget. The women never had a chance.

When dawn finally broke and the fire had been reduced to smouldering embers, the village took stock. In total, the raging inferno had claimed the hotel, three homes, John Wilson's smithy, a tavern and a carpenter's shop. The three milliners were the only human casualties.

Rumours followed that the fire was a deliberate act, likely set to drive protestant James Small from this Catholic stronghold. A second fire, this one taking hold in Small's temporary residence two months later, seemed to confirm the suspicions and sent the man fleeing from town for good. The Adjala Council expressed outrage and disgust and they offered a $5,000 reward for the conviction of the guilty party. George C. Hughes, editor of the *Cardwell Sentinel*, was equally aghast, writing: "if he [the culprit] be found, Judge Lynch will adjudicate, and hell contains no corner hot enough for him thereafter." It was his belief, and that of many others, that the culprit deserved "neither mercy in this world nor in the world to come."

Many pinned the blame on the infamous Black Donnellys of Lucan, Ontario. The seven Donnelly brothers were known as bullies with a hatred for Protestants and a long list of assaults — and murders — to their credit. Yet no one would arrest them, so frightful was their reputation. It is well known that the Donnellys were close friends of James Feheley. It is also well known that the Donnellys occasionally visited Ballycroy for some rowdy fun. Perhaps inevitably, suspicion for the fire that destroyed Small's Hotel fell upon their shoulders, as it was known several of the clan had been in the vicinity around the time of the burning. Arson certainly wouldn't have been out of character for these thugs.

In an effort to heal its wounds, the grieving village raised a headstone in memory of the deceased in the cemetery at St. James's Church in nearby Colgan. It reads: "To the memories of Mary A. Fanning, aged 32 years; Margaret H. Dakey, aged 24 years; and Bridget Burke, aged 28 years, who perished in the conflagration which, on April 29, 1875 destroyed the village of Ballycroy, this monument is erected by their afflicted relatives."

The guilty individuals were never found, and Ballycroy was never the same again. The destroyed businesses were never rebuilt, while others were shifted to Palgrave and Alliston, both of which, unlike Ballycroy, had recently been reached by the railroads. From a peak population of almost 400 in 1875, the town dwindled to 200 souls in 1881 and a mere 150 by 1900. Railways were the new lifeblood of the economy, and those towns that were unfortunate enough not to be linked were at a severe disadvantage.

The area's first business, the sawmill belonging to Samuel Beatty, was also the last. It continued to service the area even after Ballycroy had all but disappeared. The last owner was W. J. Francis, who purchased the mill in 1918 and continued its operation for another 20 years.

When the Orangeville Road (Highway 9) and the Toronto-north road (Highway 50) were straightened in the twentieth century so as to bypass Ballycroy entirely, the sleepy hamlet was turned into a virtual ghost town. The population subsequently dwindled to less than 50.

Some believe that the list of Ballycroy's misfortunes — and those of the Small family in particular — don't end here, however. On December 2, 1919, millionaire Ambrose Small, the nephew of former innkeeper James Small, disappeared in broad daylight from the streets of Toronto. He was at the height of his power and prestige at the time, without any debts or business concerns. But did he have enemies, perhaps some that dated back to his uncle's problems in Ballycroy? We'll never know, but the coincidence is tantalizing. Ambrose Small was never seen again.

Ballycroy's troubles are finally behind it. Today, it is a tranquil shadow of its former boisterous glory. In fact, it's hard to believe that this location was the scene of so much drama. Ironically, the road realignment that helped doom the community has helped preserve its remnants, protecting it from the kind of residential redevelopment that has seen so many pioneer villages destroyed. As a result, much remains to remind us of Ballycroy's past — both good and bad.

Opposite the former McClelland general store, recently rebuilt into a handsome residence, stands a weathered sign announcing Ballycroy. James Small's hotel was immediately to the right and traces of its foundations can be seen amidst a clump of trees. Farther to the right runs the old Orangeville Road, now overgrown by weeds. Less than 65 feet (20 metres) along the road, beside a private driveway, stands a workshop that was once an outbuilding of the notorious Feheley hotel.

Farther on, a careful search will reveal cement curbing and, in the fields alongside the road, several foundations. About 300 metres (325 yards) down this forlorn path is a lone surviving home standing back from the road, partially obscured by bushes.

Removed from the advance of civilization and surrounded by land with an almost timeless feel to it, Ballycroy is one of the best-preserved ghost towns in Central Ontario. It is not hard to lose yourself here; a walk down the old road feels like the distance is measured in years rather than miles. You will be transported back in history to an era when Ballycroy thrived, and you can almost sense the hopes and dreams of those who settled here — dreams that were ultimately shattered by religious violence and twists of fate.

The Ghosts of Ballycroy

Ballycroy, it seems, is not merely an abandoned village, but a real ghost town. Ghosts have been known to suddenly materialize before startled witnessed and then melt back, just as suddenly, into the silent shadows. Could the echoes of Ballycroy's violent past in fact be real — the shades of former villagers who have been unable to pass on to the afterlife and instead remain trapped in their former homesteads?

Among the hundreds of individuals who stayed in the rooms of James Small's ill-fated hotel were the three young women employed as milliners in the village hat factory. They were hard workers, kind and amiable, with full lives ahead of them. Sadly, their futures were cut short by the flames that night in 1875.

The monument in honour of the three women that the villagers erected in a local cemetery was their way of putting their grief to rest. But, according to legend, rest was something that the three milliners could not find. The ghosts of Mary Fanning, Margaret Dakey and Bridget Burke began to haunt the site of their deaths, and some claim a dark ambiance surrounds the location of the former hotel. Their spirits are said to wander the area singly, so it is unknown how many of the girls remain restless in death. It could be just one, or perhaps all three.

Regardless of their number, appearances of the ghostly milliners are often preceded by the aroma of smoke and a patch of great warmth, residual energy left over from the devastating fire that cost them their lives.

Whereas the ghostly milliners were born of tragedy, no one is certain of the origins — or even identity — of another Ballycroy ghost. One of the few original buildings to remain in Ballycroy is the former McClelland general store and hotel, now lovingly restored as a private residence. The handsome two-storey structure, itself a relic of a bygone era, is home to an unidentified woman from the past who refuses to pass on to the other side.

Ballycroy resident and *de facto* town historian Dave Bond relates the tale:

"Some time ago an elderly woman was a guest in the old

store, staying in one of the upstairs bedrooms. One night she felt a presence in the room, like a pair of eyes boring into her. The woman awoke to find an old lady, dressed in Victorian clothes and her hair in a style long out-of-date, staring down at her as she slept.

"Not knowing what to do or how to rationalize what was before her eyes, the elderly woman remained as calm as her quivering body would allow. The ghost continued to stand over her, boring into her with cold eyes. The woman began wondering what the ghost could possible want with her, and as if reading her mind, the spirit finally spoke in a cold, hollow voice: 'Why are you in my room?'

"With these words ringing in her ears, the elderly house guest was naturally startled and afraid. She clamped her eyes shut and tried to fall back to sleep, hoping that with morning's light the ghost would simply disappear. It worked. Come morning, the woman's night-time visitor was gone and she felt safe enough to leave her bed.

"When the woman told her hosts about the event and how the ghost questioned her presence in the room, she was remarkably calm. The house owners were shocked at how casually she had taken the experience, convinced that if they had seen the ghost they wouldn't have been nearly as calm. But the old woman assured them that she never felt threatened by the experience.

"'I'm 90 years old,' she said. 'What could the ghost have done to me?'"

Others have seen this ghost — presumably a former resident — over the years as well. Was it some forgotten tragedy that causes her to remain tied to the building all these years later, or is it perhaps an unusually strong affinity for the building? We'll never know.

It seems likely that both tragedy and an unusually strong affinity may be responsible for tying Ballycroy's final ghost to his haunt.

The original road west from Ballycroy to the town of Orangeville is now little more than an overgrown lane. After a brief walk, however, the shadowy form of a lone cabin suddenly appears between the dark pines. There's something oddly unsettling about the cabin, almost as if it has purposefully hidden itself away from civilization and resents any intrusion.

Dave Bond recalls that the cottage was the homestead of the Pettit family. They were simple farmers, unassuming and humble.World War I brought heartbreak to the Pettits, as the conflict did for so many families. In 1916, Chester Pettit, who grew up in the tiny three-room cabin, enlisted in the Canadian Army and was promptly shipped to France for front-line duty. He never returned home.

Or did he? Some have come away believing that his spirit haunts the cabin to this day — these authors included.

Almost 90 years after Chester's death, a young couple out to enjoy a county walk visited the former village, never anticipating the intimate connection they'd make with the past.

Leaving their car behind, they walked along the over-grown road into the bush. The ground was still hard with frost, but with the sun shining it was a beautiful day for a hike. They couldn't believe their eyes when a cottage from long ago, yet still in remarkable condition, appeared before them. Lost in their thoughts, the couple had almost walked past it.

Curiosity getting the better of them, they decided to climb in through an open window at the rear of the cabin. With only a hint of sunlight filtering in, it was almost impossible to see anything inside. After some time the woman began to feel uneasy and asked her boyfriend if they could leave. Once safely outside, she told him she had a strange feeling that they didn't belong in there and that it felt almost as though her breath was being sucked from her lungs. The couple headed back to their vehicle in silence, sure that someone — or something — wanted them out of the area.

They didn't leave before taking some photographs of their outing, however. When the film was developed, one photo stood out from the rest. This image, which was eerie and darker in tone than the others, revealed the spectral image of a man not from this time. Their experience at the cabin began to make sense. Could the ghost in the photo be Chester Pettit? Had the young couple inadvertently disturbed Pettit by trespassing in his domain? Their walk that March day became a walk into the past that they would never forget.

And perhaps we're intended to never forget Ballycroy either, because it clings desperately to life. Time seems to stand still in this ghost town, and as long as it remains so, it seems likely that the spirits of its troubled past will be content to remain there.

Chapter 2
Keenansville

Location: Follow Highway 9 west from Highway 400, turning north on County Road 15. Take this road north to the 7th line, and then turn west once more. A stone plaque stands at the intersections of old Marie and Victoria streets, telling in brief the story of Keenansville.

Driving Time from Toronto: 1 hour.

Keenansville was once a prosperous mill town.

Many of us are immigrants to this New World, and most others can claim ancestors who, at one point or another, came to this country from elsewhere. And yet, do we ever stop to consider the travails our pioneering forefathers encountered when coming to Canada? For those of us who made the move in modern times, it was relatively easy. But for those who came a century or two before, things were far different. It makes their decision to leave the country of their birth all the more courageous.

All immigrants, regardless of their life stories and the date of their arrival, have one thing in common: they left their native homes to make a better life for future generations. Keenansville was founded upon this desire for a better life.

Famine gripped Ireland in the 1820s. Tens of thousands starved to death, and an equal number immigrated to North America in search of new land, new hope and a new beginning. Among those who fled the Emerald Isle were John and Eleanor Keenan and their ten children, who turned their backs on their ancestral home in June of 1825. Six weeks later they arrived in Quebec, and autumn found them in York (now Toronto).

Keenan was offered land at the present intersection of King and Yonge streets, but he turned it down. There was an Indian belief that Lake Ontario rose and fell on a seven-year cycle, and it was said that at high tide the waters would wash up against King Street (despite the fact that the Great Lakes are not subject to tidal effects). Keenan heard these tales and believed them. A newcomer to Canada, he was perhaps naïve about its natural order. Concerned that his land would be inundated when the waters inevitably rose once more, he turned down the government's offer and instead accepted a lot in the wilds of Adjala Township (in south Simcoe County, north of Toronto). The land he refused would have been worth a small fortune just a few years later.

Adjala at the time was largely uninhabited. There were no roads offering access into its wilds, no farmsteads to break the monotony of dark forest, no settlements in which to find companionship or sanctuary. It was a true frontier, wild and unforgiving. But beneath the harshness, Adjala also offered prosperity. The soil was rich and fertile, the forest provided rich resources, and the strong-flowing waterways were ideally suited to power early industry. It was the new beginning that the Keenans and so many other Irish immigrants had hoped for.

John Keenan established a farmstead along Bailey Creek, a tributary of the Nottawasaga River, and was soon joined by others. For many years, settlement took the form of scattered farms in the midst of wilderness, and nothing more. But slowly a true community began to emerge, taking the name Keenansville after the area's first settler.

Keenansville had two streets: Victoria, running east and west, and Marie, running north and south. At the southern extremity of the village, Marie Street curved down a steep hill and became Keenan's Lane, so-called because it marked the boundary of the Keenan Farm.

The community's commercial core was located along Marie Street, where a succession of businesses huddled close together. The most prominent of these was the general store run by George Hughes. Far more than simply a mercantile, the store was also home to the post office, the village bank, a telegraph office (the telegraph line ran along the seventh line of Tecumseh from Bradford) and office for a newspaper called the *Simcoe Observer* (later the *Cardwell Sentinel*).

Hughes used his four-page weekly paper, which at one time had a circulation of 1,000, to advocate on behalf of the community and serve as its moral compass. His editorials could be scathing at times. When the Bailey Creek Bridge was in need of repair, for example, he angrily demanded that, "the Keenansville path master see to the dangerous state of the bridge ... if not, we'll see to him."

Keenansville's post office was established in 1855. Originally, mail arrived via stage from Bolton, but after the railway reached Tottenham in the 1870s, the postmaster would ride over to the station to pick up and deliver letters and parcels.

Just south of Hughes's business was the Keenansville schoolhouse, a frame structure built in the 1840s. At one point it had an enrolment of more than 50 students, though a figure closer to 30 was the norm. Just beyond the school was a huge barnlike building that was home to the annual

Adjala Agricultural Fair, one of the largest social events in the township.

Alongside Bailey Creek, at the base of the Marie Street hill, stood twin mills that were the foundation of the community's economy. On the south side of the road was a sawmill that provided lumber for local needs. During winter months, ice was harvested from the millpond's frozen surface and stored in icehouses for use throughout the year. In the summer, the millpond was popular with boaters, especially for romantic dalliances.

Opposite the sawmill, on the north side of the road, towered a three-storey woollen mill. This mill was of particular importance to Keenansville. Its full-time workforce included three weavers, four carders, five framers and a spinner, marking it as the largest employer in the village by a large margin. Because its yarn was very popular it needed lots of wool so most area farmers kept large flocks of sheep.

Both mills were owned by John Brown, undoubtedly the wealthiest man in town. His beautiful home stood on the hill directly above the woollen mill so that he could literally oversee his businesses.

Keenansville grew rapidly, in large measure due to the mills' success, and the prosperity they provided. By 1866, the bustling town boasted a population of 300 and more than a dozen stores and services. In addition to Hughes's store and the mills, there were two blacksmith shops, three shoe emporiums, four wagon factories and a pair of hotels.

Both hotels were known for their lively revelry, but Moore's Ontario House Hotel took the concept of drunken revelry to new heights. The alcohol flowed fast and cheap in the bar, leading to booze-induced brawls that spilled out onto the street, seemingly on a nightly basis. Hughes railed against the "notorious ... and unseemly brawls" in his scathing commentaries, helping Ontario House earn a justifiably seedy reputation. The problem grew so serious that Keenansville had to hire a pair of police constables to combat the misbehaviour that centred on the hotel.

Keenansville, on the eve of the 1880s, was at the pinnacle of its fortunes. There were unsavoury elements, to be sure, a dark underbelly of which most respectable citizens were embarrassed. But it was also the largest and most prosperous community in Adjala Township, a thriving community with many businesses and an industry of wide renown.

Robert Keenan, and the others who had fled destitution in Ireland years before, had established a town that shone like a beacon for future immigrants who might have their own aspirations for a better life, demonstrating that dreams really could come true in the New World. Perhaps understandably, its residents looked confidently towards the future.

Unfortunately, it all proved to be little more than a cruel illusion. The confidence of the townsfolk was grossly misplaced: in reality Keenansville had no future. Instead, through a combination of events, it died and became a ghost town. The nails in Keenansville's coffin were hammered in slowly, one after another, over the next three decades.

The first blow to the town's fortunes was struck in 1877, when the Hamilton and North-Western Railway passed Keenansville by, electing to run its lines through nearby Tottenham instead. It was a devastating blow. Railways were the new lifeblood of the economy, and those communities that were unfortunate enough not to be linked to them were at a severe disadvantage. Inevitably, industry gravitated towards railway lines as a means of transporting goods to distant markets.

Gradually, most businesses in Keenansville began to migrate towards Tottenham or closed up shop completely. Within a decade of the railway's arrival, three of the wagon shops, a blacksmith and several cobblers had either left for greener pastures or simply thrown in the towel. The sawmill along Bailey Creek was reduced to running only on a limited basis, whenever local needs demanded. One hotel boarded up its windows and locked its doors. By the turn of the century there were no more than a handful of businesses remaining in town. These included the general store, the wagon factory and carpentry shop operated by John Cahoon and the Ontario House Hotel.

The Brown mill continued to operate, but it became increasingly difficult to turn a profit. The cost of transporting its wares by wagon to the railway station at Tottenham meant that it was almost impossible to compete on an equal basis with other woollen mills across Ontario. Still, the mill retained a reputation for fine quality wool, and demand remained high.

In a way, the Ontario House Hotel was responsible for its own demise. Subsisting almost exclusively on the proceeds from its lively bar, it became well known as an establishment where whiskey and rowdiness were served hand-in-hand. Many townsfolk grew tired of the unseemly drunken behaviour and become willing converts to the temperance movement that campaigned against the evils of alcohol. Under pressure from temperance advocates, Adjala Township began to give out liquor licenses less liberally and crack down on offensive establishments. When Ontario House inevitably lost its license, owner James Egan recognised that he could no longer operate the hotel profitably and promptly closed down.

Its demise was probably past due, because Egan moonlighted as village undertaker. Bodies were prepared for burial in a small room off the bar, much to the discomfort of his patrons. For many years even the hardest drinkers had grumbled about throwing back their whiskey while corpses were laid out only one room away.

After Ontario House, the next to go was the general store. George Morrow, who ran the largest wagon factory in town, purchased the store in his twilight years as a means of sustaining himself in retirement. When he passed away in 1908 at the age of 70 years, no one took up the mantle. The store, which was only doing minimal business by now, closed for good.

The most devastating blow to Keenansville came when the Brown Woollen Mill was forced out of business by modern synthetic substitutes to wool. Its spindles ceased turning just prior to World War I, which not only put several locals out of work, but also eliminated a source of guaranteed income for area farmers who kept flocks of sheep solely to supply the mill.

The loss of the community's largest industry represented the last nail in Keenansville's coffin, effectively sealing its fate. Within a few years, nothing was left except for scattered farms and decaying ruins. Keenansville was wrapped securely in a ghostly shroud. So completely had it disappeared that by the time we visited, we were surprised by how few relics of the past remained to be seen.

Recently, modern homes have begun to appear along the village's former streets, bringing an element of life back to the community. But ghosts of the nineteenth-century village still exist, for those who are willing to lift back the cloak of ages and who know where to look.

At the intersection of Marie and Victoria streets there is the plaque commemorating the ghost town of Keenansville. On either side of the stone, lilac bushes line the street, a sure sign of the locations where pioneer homes and businesses once stood. Just to the east is the old Morrow general store, a large, brown clapboard building that is today a private residence.

The Brown residence still stands atop the hill overlooking Bailey Creek, though it is partially obscured by trees and difficult to see. In its day it would have been a large, extravagant home worthy of the richest man in town, though it's now dwarfed by new homes being erected nearby.

Brown's millpond, just south of the bridge spanning Bailey Creek, is still visible. Along its shore stood the sawmill. No evidence of the towering woollen mill, which occupied land on the northeast side of the bridge, remains. The fields have reclaimed the site and now wildflowers bloom where once an industry thrived.

As we leaned over the guardrail of Bailey Creek Bridge, we could almost hear the spectral din of activity that centred upon this placid waterway. Or were we just falling prey to the fertile imaginings of our own minds?

It's hard to say for certain, because past and present collide at Keenansville.

Chapter 3
Hagerman's Corners

Location: Hagerman's Corners lies in Markham, part of the Greater Toronto Area, and is centred upon the intersection of what is today Kennedy Road and 14th Avenue.
Driving Time from Toronto: 20 minutes.

Not all ghost towns lie abandoned along some country road. Many villages ceased to exist when they were drowned by an onrushing wave of suburbia. More than a century ago, residents of the many pioneer hamlets that made up Markham could never have imagined the growth that would follow. This growth has been so great that many of these villages have been swallowed up by what is today a modern city. In the process they have lost their individual identities. Roads, suburbs, shopping centres and industrial parks have smothered these once-thriving communities, oftentimes erasing all evidence of their existence.

Hagerman's Corners, located in Markham, just north of Toronto, has all but disappeared today. Save for a few remnants, there is nothing to remind us that a once-thriving pioneer community existed at the corner of Kennedy Road and 14th Avenue. As thoroughly as any backwoods hamlet can be swallowed up by encroaching forest, Hagerman's Corners has been swallowed up by urban development. It is a ghosted community.

The story of this little hamlet begins in the late eighteenth century with John Hagemann (later anglicized to Hagerman), a native of Hamburg, Germany. Hagerman, along with several hundred other Germans led by William Berczy, fled poor conditions at home and immigrated to the New World. They originally took up land in New York State's Mohawk Valley, establishing farms and places of business.

Many found their new homes unsatisfactory and in 1796 petitioned the government of Upper Canada (Ontario) for land grants, specifically in Markham Township. Eager for settlers to help tame the wilds and build the foundations of civilization, Lieutenant-Governor John Graves Simcoe quickly agreed to the request. John Hagerman was one of those who put in for land, and he drew Lot 6 of Concession 5.

Unfortunately, he died before ever seeing it. It would be up to his son and sole heir, 14-year-old Nicholas, to claim this land. He and his family made the journey from New York, imagining a land of bounty and prosperity. They were likely sadly disappointed when they first set eyes upon their new home. Markham Township was at the time an imposing wilderness, and settlers were relatively few, thanks largely to the sheer isolation of the region. The roads of the day, such as

The Hagerman's Corners Public School is a grand structure typical of the Victorian era, surviving today as a reminder of a former farming community.

they were, more properly would be termed tracks and had a habit of turning into expanses of axle-deep mud in the rain. On the best of days it was possible to travel only about 12 miles.

But even the relative backwardness of the region could not dim Nicholas Hagerman's enthusiasm. An able and eager farmer, he would make good in this new land and fulfill his father's dream. Luck was on his side. The land John Hagerman had drawn occupied a strategic location at the intersection of two important thoroughfares. Crossroads such as this invariably became the centre of busy hamlets, and land in close proximity became highly valuable. Oftentimes landholders would subdivide roadside portions of their farms, turn them into village lots, and sell them for a tidy profit.

That's exactly what Hagerman did when craftsmen, merchants and other farmers joined him at the crossroads. What began as a trickle of settlers turned into a flood between 1820 and 1840, when many peasant farmers from Ireland and Scotland were forced off their farms by absentee landowners. But like his father, who never got to see his land grant, Nicholas Hagerman did not live long enough to see the village take off. It wouldn't be until a few years after his death in 1838 that the community really found its legs.

By the 1850s the village — named Hagerman's Corners in honour of its founder — could boast a hotel, two stores, a shoemaker, two cabinetmakers, several other craftsmen, a church, a school and a population of about 100.

The school served children from all over the district, including those from the neighbouring village of Milliken, some four miles distant. One of the students from this one-room schoolhouse, Clarence Augustus Chant, would rise to national fame as "the father of Canadian astronomy." Born on May 31, 1865, Chant emerged from a humble background to become one of the most respected and influential scientists in the nation. He taught from 1891 to 1935 at the University of Toronto, where he organized the Department of Astronomy and, perhaps more importantly, was the driving force behind Toronto's famed Dunlop Observatory.

Hagerman's Corners had two mercantiles. Village general

stores were among the most important facilities in a pioneer community, serving as small-town department stores where one could purchase anything one might need. They were also social centres in a way, serving as places where townsfolk would stop to share news and gossip and form friendships. The first of the two stores was opened by William McPherson in the late 1830s, the second by James Fairless in the 1850s. The latter would later be known as Galloway's and remained in business well into the 1960s, the last of the village businesses to board its windows and close up shop.

At the heart of the village, both figuratively and literally, was the quaintly named Beehive Hotel. It was founded by John Webber in the 1850s and was initially called Webber's Hotel. The proprietor was something of a hotel magnate, running several other inns in the township. In 1869, his daughter, Matilda Jane, married a native of Hagerman's Corners, a gentleman named Orson Hemmingway. As a wedding gift, ownership of Webber's Hotel was passed to the young couple.

Orson Hemmingway came from a local farming family and had no experience in the hospitality industry. Yet, he was a quick learner and proved himself an able businessman. "As a hotel-keeper," noted a contemporary account, "he is found courteous and obliging, and is everything else to be desired." One of his first actions was to change the name to the Beehive Hotel, though no one seems to know where the inspiration for the name lay.

The History of Toronto and York County, published in

1885, noted that the Beehive was a well-appointed hotel, a place "where every accommodation is afforded to the traveling community." This claim showed considerable artistic license on the writers' part, however. The truth is, like most rural hotels, the Beehive had only modest accommodations and only a small portion of its business came from overnight guests. The real money lay in serving up beer and whiskey in the ever-lively barroom. Whether it was parched travellers or locals in search of camaraderie, the bar was rarely less than full.

Whatever name it went by, the hotel played a prominent role in local affairs. Not only did men congregate here to relax, tell tall tales and share news, but it also served as an unofficial community hall where people could meet to discuss matters of importance. No building was more central to the community's sense of identity than the hotel. It came to define Hagerman's Corners.

Orson and Matilda Jane Hemmingway had a large family of five daughters and three sons, one of whom, Thomas, would later take over the hotel. Thomas carried the business forward well into the twentieth century, and it was he who was responsible for the quirky sign that old-timers remember dangling from the front porch. It read:

> *Within this hive we're much alive*
> *Good liquor makes us funny*
> *So if you're dry come in and try*
> *The flavour of our honey*

Though Orson and Thomas Hemmingway were important figures in the community, another Hemmingway loomed even larger — quite literally — in town lore. The most famous member of this lineage was Moses Hemmingway, an almost legendary figure around these parts, with a larger-than-life reputation to match his giant-sized build.

The Hemmingways, true to their Scottish Highland roots, were all physically imposing individuals, known for their strength and physical endurance.

It was a characteristic that certainly came in handy when carving homesteads out of the wilderness of North America.

Moses, however, was the biggest of the lot. Born on a nearby farm in 1809, he grew into a veritable ox of a man. Even while still a teenager, he already stood as tall as most grown men and was just as powerful. When fully mature, Moses was said to be the strongest man in Markham and his hands were reputed to be the size of spade heads. People watched in amazement as he swung his seven-and-a-half pound axe as if it were a hatchet. It was said he could fell a tree faster than any man alive. He was a gentle giant, however, and far more thoughtful than his brutish appearance would suggest.

When Upper Canada was wracked by conflict in 1837, the Hemmingways remained true to the Crown, rather than throwing in their lot with William Lyon Mackenzie and his rebels. Moses was courted by the insurgents on account of his prodigious strength and skill with the musket, but he refused all entreaties and threatened anyone with violence if they talked of treason in his presence. He refused to accept the path of violence as a means of effecting change.

For six decades Moses Hemmingway peacefully worked his farm and prospered, but the bodies of even the strongest men eventually give out. On March 15, 1875, at the age of 66 years, he died. His legend, however, outlived him for many decades and people were still speaking of this impressive figure of a man when Hagerman's Corners began its slow spiral into oblivion during the early years of the twentieth century.

It was a tenacious little community, however, and clung to life far longer than many other farming hamlets in the area. Despite never being large or particularly significant, much of Hagerman's Corners survived intact until the 1970s, a rural island in an advancing sea of urbanism. Finally, grudgingly, it gave way to the relentless pressure of suburban growth and disappeared. Modern strip malls and subdivisions have since replaced farmhouses and fields of grain at what is still a busy crossroads.

Yet some small vestiges of the former hamlet remain. The pioneer cemetery is still there, though the church is long gone. The plot is pitifully small, demonstrating just how diminutive Hagerman's Corners truly was, and the aged headstones seem out of place amidst the sea of modernity. There are also several 1850s-era homes to be found along Kennedy Road and 14th Avenue, most notably one that belonged to Nicholas Hagerman Jr., the grandson of John Hagerman. This attractive brick home, which dates back to 1853, is wedged in amidst a townhouse subdivision and was very nearly torn down to make way for modern development. Thankfully, sane heads prevailed and the historic home has been beautifully restored, designated as a Markham Heritage Home, and awarded a plaque that details the local significance of the Hagerman family.

In its day, Hagerman's Corners was a lively hamlet with a strong sense of identity, but 30-odd years after its last gasp the village has been all but wiped away. Even memories are fading fast. Few people in cosmopolitan Markham have ever heard of Hagerman's Corners today, let alone recognize that for 150 years it was a distinct community.

Whatever echoes of Hagerman's Corners that might remain at the intersection of Kennedy Road and 14th Avenue are now drowned out by the roar of constant traffic.

Chapter 4
Glenville

Location: Glenville is located along Highway 9, roughly midway between Highway 400 and Newmarket. Glenville Road, announced by a fading sign, is on the north side of the road directly opposite Dufferin.

Driving Time from Toronto: 30 minutes.

Imagine hitching up the team and taking a ride along a rugged but pleasant country lane called Mulock Road, which leads through some of the most picturesque scenery in northern York County. First we pass the beautiful grounds and country residence of Sir William Mulock, Member of Parliament for North York, riding through his shaded walnut groves and flowering apple orchards, which will captivate us with their scent. We keep going to enter the Gamble Bush, with its winding roads and exquisite scenery. Then, after passing some fine country estates belonging to Toronto's elite, we reach the high point of the land for a spectacular view of the surrounding countryside. We stop and take in the surprising panorama of the valley below with the thriving mill village of Glenville nestled in its fold, a little community in which so much history unfolded.

In the earliest years of the nineteenth century, the vast forests of York Region lured industrious men into the wilderness in search of their fortunes. These men scoured the area for suitable sawmill sites, and once they located one, began vigorously cutting down trees. Timber was like gold at the time, and in particular pine, which was used to make masts for the Royal Navy.

The forgotten hamlet of Glenville was one of many communities in Ontario that owed its existence to a sawmill.

In 1807 William Lloyd, a Pennsylvanian Quaker with all the famed industriousness of his brethren, and who would later found the village of Lloydtown, happened upon a forested gully just west of Yonge Street. The site was perfect for a sawmill — it had a ready supply of water to power the machinery, was thickly wooded with great stands of pine, and was within easy distance of Yonge Street, then the only link to York (Toronto) and therefore the region's commercial artery.

Lloyd recognized a good thing when he saw it and built a sawmill on the southern of two ponds. As happened with most mills, a small village slowly developed around it. The first people to follow Lloyd were workers employed in his business enterprise, but as the forest was cleared and the rich soil lying beneath it was revealed, farmers were attracted to the area as well. Many of the early settlers were Scottish immigrants, with names like Bolton, Graham, Sommerville and Brodie, so it was appropriate that the community adopted a Highland-sounding name.

Glenville soon came to the attention of two of Ontario's most prominent entrepreneurs, John Cawthra and William Roe. Both began thriving businesses in the newly founded hamlet, their success feeding Glenville's rapid growth.

Cawthra, born in 1792 and the son of one of York's richest merchants, was himself an accomplished businessman. Already the owner of a profitable store and distillery in nearby Newmarket, in 1836 he built a gristmill in Glenville on the pond north of Lloyd's. The mill was joined by a distillery owned by William Roe that made whiskey selling for a mere 12 cents per gallon. Such distilleries typically operated alongside gristmills since they relied upon cleansed grain for making their alcohol. One of the first settlers in Newmarket, Roe was for many years engaged in the fur trade there, but began branching out into other concerns, such as stagecoach and steamship operations, as the community lost its central role in that industry.

In addition to Cawthra's mill and Roe's distillery, other businesses migrated to Glenville. As they did, the population swelled so that by the middle of the century the village counted more than 100 inhabitants. There were two inns in town, sating the thirst of locals and tending to the needs of travellers. Glenville is situated at the bottom of a small hill on an escarpment that would have challenged early travellers, so it was a logical place to rest and water horses, and to provide the passengers with a drink, a meal or a bed and perhaps all three. One hotel was called the Sand Bank, owned by John Hare; the other was the Central Hotel, with Charles Brodie as proprietor. As well as running a hotel, Brodie also served as one of two blacksmiths in town.

Additionally, Glenville consisted of two general stores, one of which was also home to a felt hat-making shop, Christopher Scott's blanket- and carpet-making business, two coopers who made barrels for whiskey and flour and a temperance hall in which people spoke out against the ills of whiskey. It wasn't until 1900 that the village gained a post office, which operated out of the home of then-miller Samuel Waldock.

William Lloyd didn't remain in Glenville long enough to see it prosper, however. Infused with wanderlust, he sold his sawmill and moved on to new frontiers. The business's new operator was Ellis Hughes, a fellow Pennsylvanian Quaker who had previously owned a sawmill at Holland Landing. Hughes has an interesting place in history. His first mill provided the lumber for the construction of the mysterious and beautiful Sharon Temple, a house of worship built by a divergent Quaker sect and now the premier historical attraction in the Newmarket area.

After purchasing the Lloyd Mill, Hughes undertook extensive renovations, both in the building and its machinery. The most important change he made was upgrading the obsolete equipment with the more modern "muley mill," in which the frame remained stationary and only the blade itself moved up and down (as with a jig saw). This made for greater efficiency and increased profits.

All this growth and prosperity occurred during turbulent times in Canada's history. In the 1830s discontent with the corrupt colonial government was widespread across Ontario — so much so that people began to whisper of rebellion. In December 1837, the pent-up frustration exploded in armed revolt that saw hundreds of farmers and craftsmen march towards Toronto. The rebellion was crushed, but its leaders remained at large and the embers of discontent continued to smoulder.

Shortly after these events had unfolded, the citizens of Glenville began construction of a schoolhouse. Mrs. Thomas Heaslip, a widowed Loyalist woman who lived nearby, caught wind of the frenzied activity and grew suspicious. Somehow, she got it into her head that rebels were building a fort in Glenville and sent word to the authorities in Toronto. Several officers were dispatched to investigate the claim. They interrogated villagers, searched private property for arms and ammunition, and treated one and all with the type of contempt usually reserved for criminals.

Naturally enough, this officious behaviour raised tensions in the village. Tempers finally snapped when the officers ordered one particular farmer, a man who apparently had connections to rebel leader Jesse Lloyd of Lloydtown, to hand over his gun. The farmer adamantly refused. He

When Alexander Hall started as schoolmater of Glenville, he learned the difficulties of imposing one's authority as a rural teacher, most of whom were rarely older than the students.

would allow them to search his property, but he would not allow his gun to be confiscated. When all attempts at persuasion and threats had failed to dislodge the man, the officers retreated to a safe distance to load their pistols, plan a course of action and prepare themselves for a bloody end to the standoff. Just as the soldiers were about to storm the farmhouse, cooler heads prevailed and the attack was called off. Perhaps the men realized that a farmer's old hunting musket simply wasn't worth their lives. Having found no evidence of rebellious activity, the officers mounted up and beat a hasty retreat to Toronto.

The Glenville school that was at the centre of this drama was hardly fortresslike in stature or appearance. It was a simple log structure, measuring 16 feet by 20 feet, with boards along the walls that were used as desks and split-rail benches for children to sit on. There was nothing threatening or imposing about it. This building, which had caused so much fuss that it had almost cost a farmer his life, soon passed into history. In 1855 it was replaced with a new frame schoolhouse.

Enrolment in those early days was between 35 and 50 students, peaking in the winter when the older boys, some as old as 22, were released from farm duties until spring. These husky young men engaged in almost daily brawls and it took an able-bodied man to run the Glenville School. One unfortunate teacher was actually thrown through the window by his students and promptly quit. Another, who attempted to discipline a brawny lad, found himself overpowered by the boy and his brother and the whip turned on him.

One of the more successful at taming the students was a teacher named Alexander Hall. When he arrived for his first day of school, Hall found the children had arranged a warm reception for him. The front door had been completely blocked by firewood, reaching as high as the roof. It was meant as a warning — the students were in charge here. The young teacher was undeterred, however. He found an open window and ushered the students inside. Except for the boys, that is. It was their task to restack the firewood, which they did under the watchful eye of the schoolmaster. If a student slacked, he was driven to greater effort with the bruising crack of a birch rod. After this demonstration of authority, Hall had no further trouble with the students.

The citizens of Glenville were God-fearing, so they erected a Methodist church shortly after the new school was built. The village church was a profoundly important building, serving as the social heart of the community. In addition to religious services, it hosted town meetings, the school's annual Christmas concert, craft and bake sales and strawberry parties organized by local women, oftentimes raising money for charity.

Throughout its existence, the little church remained remarkably unchanged. Orma Faris, 90 years old and a life-long resident of the community, remembers only one cause for significant renovations. "One day, a wedding service was taking place in the church. The bride entered and everyone stood up, as people do, to watch as she walked down the aisle. Suddenly, the floor gave way! Now, there's no basement, just a foot's space and then ground, so no one was seriously hurt. And of course, the wedding continued, but it wasn't the perfect day most women imagine."

Glenville lasted as long as the mills did, but when they fell silent so too did the once-bustling community. Ellis Hughes's sawmill was razed by fire in 1898, but since most of the worthwhile lumber had long since been cut it was never rebuilt. Cawthra's gristmill lasted two decades longer, but met a similar fiery end in 1916. There was still a need in the community for a facility to grind grain, so Fred Webster built a small mill to replace the one that had been destroyed. Like its predecessors, it too met a fiery end, burning down in 1934.

"I remember that day vividly," recalls 88-year old Russell Somerville, a lifelong resident of Glenville who proudly claims ancestors among the earliest residents of the community. "I was a student at the time, and the mill was still smoking by the time we went to school in the morning. We kids wanted nothing to do with our studies — we wanted to see the action. So our teacher, Eliza Owens, a wonderful lady, finally gave up on her lesson and took us down to the mill to watch the remains of the mill burn. It was an exciting day for a young kid."

Unfortunately, when the mill went up in smoke, so too did the future of Glenville.

After the mills were gone, the blacksmiths and hotels quickly closed as well, and the village stagnated. Within a decade all of the businesses had disappeared, having migrated to towns with brighter futures. The one-room schoolhouse was the last non-residential building to close, graduating its final class in 1955.

There was a time when people thought that Glenville would become a rural haven for Toronto families. "In this picturesque part of the Township folk from the city are coming to buy home sites and some day Glenville will see a new kind of population come," predicted the *Aurora Banner* enthusiastically on February 3, 1939. It was not to be, however. The suburban boom never arrived and Glenville languished in obscurity.

When Highway 9 was straightened it bypassed the little hamlet, thereby preserving its remains as a timeless island of tranquility in a sea of encroaching modernity. As a result, though the village of Glenville has largely been reclaimed by the forests that once fuelled its rapid growth, some reminders of the village's past are still evident.

The old church, now privately owned and used only for occasional weddings, is the most obvious remnant, standing right at the village crossroads. Glenville's once busy main street today resembles a country lane. It leads into a valley where Cawthra's mill once stood, though the pond has long since dried up. The remains of Lloyd's millpond, half of which was buried by the construction of Highway 9, is immediately south, astride Dufferin Street.

Valley of the Dead Man's Bones

If you happen to be driving west from Newmarket along Highway 9 on a rainy, foggy day you might want to take extra care as you come around a bend in the road as it skirts a pond. An eerie mist rises slowly from the dark water studded with rotting tree stumps. There is something forbidding — almost ominous — about its appearance, and perhaps unsurprisingly, many people have lost their lives at this corner in the past. Even though there is a guardrail in place today to prevent vehicles from going off the road, an aura of imminent danger still lingers. It's almost as if the pond cries out to passing cars, attempting to pull the vehicles and their passengers to their murky deaths.

The pond's name is suitably spine chilling — as far back as anyone can remember it has been known as the Valley of the Dead Man's Bones. Why would anyone give this place a name laced with tragedy and horror?

According to several written accounts and local Glenville lore, human remains were found in the valley sometime during the nineteenth century by workers at William Lloyd's sawmill. Most people believe that this tragic soul met his or her death by foul play. It's possible that the individual had been brutally attacked and the body disposed of in the murky waters of the pond.

We have a false impression that our pioneer history was free of the lawlessness, violence and crime that characterized America's development during the same period. However, the truth is very different. Early Ontario was full of shady characters. Guns could be carried openly until late in the nineteenth century and were used regularly. With booze running fast and cheap, drunken behaviour ran rampant. Ontario even had outlaws, bandits and organized crime gangs.

So perhaps the unfortunate person was dealt a tragic death at the hands of someone who remains unknown to us today. Or maybe the death was simply the result of a tragic, perhaps drunken, accident. We will never know.

More recently, since the arrival of the automobile, people began referring to the stretch of road that bends around the former millpond as Dead Man's Curve. With the new era came a new story.

Many years ago, a young man, tired from a long day at work, was racing towards the comforts of his home. It was dark and his headlights reflected off a haze of falling snow, reducing visibility to near zero. Yet on he sped, eager to get home.

He would never arrive. The young man failed to see the turn until it was too late. There wasn't enough time to brake. The vehicle sailed off the road, crumpled as it bounced several times down the hillside, and plunged into the pond. The driver was either already dead or unconscious and drowned as the car sank into the freezing depths. Either way, he died a tragic death.

Several decades later, another person driving along this same stretch of road nearly suffered the curse of Dead Man's Curve.

Wendy had resided in the area for many years, during which time she had heard a lot about Dead Man's Curve and often wondered about the origin of this haunting name. But in truth, she never put much stock in the curses and hauntings rumoured to be tied to the spot. It was folklore, nothing more.

After a busy morning spent in Toronto and with many

things playing on her troubled mind, Wendy strangely found herself driving on Highway 9, a road that would not normally lie along her route home. Visibility was greatly reduced by thick fog, so she was taking extra care to keep the truck on the road. It seemed that with each passing mile, the closer she drove towards Dead Man's curve, the fog became thicker. Soon Wendy could barely see at all. Suddenly, to her horror, the red glare of traffic lights appeared out of the murk immediately ahead. She frantically hit the brakes. As the wheels fought to find a grip on the slick asphalt and the truck slid towards the intersection, Wendy believed that her life was over. Her one thought was that she was going to leave her only child, and she worried that her death would forever scar her daughter.

She was filled with relief as the truck finally squealed to a stop just before the intersection, and just as cars began to pull out in front of her. Disaster had been narrowly averted. Wendy felt that something or someone was watching over her that day, saving her life. Incredibly, this was exactly one year since the passing of her brother. Could he have been watching over Wendy, making sure that she would not be another casualty on this deadly stretch of road?

For Wendy, Dead Man's Curve is not just another story from folklore now, it is also one for her to tell. And she no longer questions the origin of the name, instinctively understanding the fear and respect with which successive generations have viewed the area.

"My father told me about the Valley of the Dead Man's

Bones," recalls 88-year-old Russell Somerville. "Years ago, when he was young or maybe even his father was young, a body was mysteriously found down there. There are strange stories about how it got to be there, but no one knows."

Mr. Somerville is right. We don't know, and we'll likely never know whether the tales behind the valley's chilling name are fact or fiction, or whether the spirits of those who may have died there remain tied to their watery grave, as some believe. And perhaps it is better that way — we need a little mystery in our lives, something to fuel our imaginations.

If you happen to be driving along this stretch of Highway 9, listen closely because you just might hear cries from long ago — like the sirens of Greek myth luring you to your doom.

Chapter 5
Swords/Maple Lake Station

Location: Swords is found in Parry Sound District. Exit Highway 400 at Highway 141 and drive 16 km east. Turn north onto Swords/Tally-Ho Road and follow its winding surface until you see a weathered general store on the left and a recreational trail bisecting the roadway. This is Swords.
Driving Time from Toronto: 2.5 hours.

The story of Swords (originally called Maple Lake Station) is intertwined with that of the family after which it was named. True, many others contributed to the community's development and to the tapestry of everyday life within the quiet hamlet, but none had their fingers in as many pies as did the Sword family itself. They were farmers, lumbermen, postmasters, proprietors of the general store, owners of Maple Lake Hotel, stagecoach operators and more. No other family was as important to putting Swords on the map and to spurring its development from a collection of wilderness farms into a bustling mill village.

The Sword clan originally hailed from Scotland, but in

the 1850s they immigrated to Glengarry Township, Ontario, a region heavily populated by their kinsmen. There, in addition to farming, Thomas Sword gained his introduction into the timber industry, working in bush camps felling trees during the long, cold winters. The family remained in eastern Ontario long enough to see several children born and ultimately wed there, but in time they grew disenchanted with a steady migration of French settlers from Quebec into the township, which changed its cultural makeup. As a result, many Scottish settlers decided to uproot once more, and the Swords were no different. Their new destination was Parry Sound District.

Thomas Sword arrived in Christie Township in 1870 with his wife and their children David, John and Margaret. Unlike many early settlers, he wasn't dismayed by the dense forests and thin soil that made agriculture so difficult in the northern reaches. It was never his intention to make his livelihood entirely from farming. Rather, he would earn his living from the trees themselves. Thomas Sword was a logging foreman, one of the best. His services were in demand by large logging companies all across the Muskoka–Parry Sound region, and beyond. In fact, his reputation spread as far south as Michigan and as far west as British Columbia.

When the family arrived, they found a land heavily forested and largely unsettled. The road that would later be called the Swords/Tally-Ho Road twisted into the dark interior of Christie Township, around rocks and lakes, over streams and marshes. There were few farms along its length, perhaps three or four, and these were little more than clearings with a few acres of crops growing amid massive tree stumps. It was a wild, uncivilized — and to many settlers, uninspiring — tract of land. But Thomas Sword knew trees meant money, and where there was money to be made industry was sure to follow.

He was right. As early as the 1880s, railway and lumber magnate J. R. Booth was planning to run a railway from Ottawa to Parry Sound, passing through the very wilderness that Thomas Sword and his family had settled. When Booth's Ottawa, Arnprior & Parry Sound Railway (OA&PS) was completed in 1896, it was the longest railway ever built and owned by a single individual. Its impact upon the Maple Lake region was immediate: seemingly overnight, the makings of a village sprouted up around the tracks and its humble flag station. This village was known as Maple Lake Station.

Thomas Sword, the experienced lumberman, was involved in the process from the start. He realized that with the arrival of the railway, the untapped potential of the forests around Maple Lake could finally be fully exploited. Trees could be cut by the thousand and shipped quickly and easily to the insatiable markets of the United States. Sword became a founding shareholder in the Long Lake Lumber Company, which purchased significant tracts of land at the south end of Maple Lake and raised a large steam-powered sawmill on its shores. Soon, the woods were ringing with the sounds of dozens of axes biting into trees, and the constant buzz of the sawmill echoed across the lake's placid surface.

From the start, the mill at Maple Lake was a large enterprise that operated year round. To cater to the millhands and their families who would live in this isolated setting, the Long Lake Lumber Company built a general store and several cabins along the railway tracks.

The area's economy was heavily dependent upon lumbering. In the poor soil, farmers were hard-pressed to grow more than their families needed to survive, and therefore had little surplus to sell. Most of their income came from winter lumbering, either in the employ of the Ludgate Lumber Company, a large lumber enterprise that operated in the Parry Sound region or on their own woodlots, felling trees that they then sold to the mill. The smooth surface of the frozen lake provided the easiest route for hauling logs to the mill, far easier than hauling them over the rolling terrain and through the thick woods. On a good day one could see up to 30 teams of horses pulling logs across Maple Lake, some coming from as far as 15 or 20 miles away.

The Sword clan was deeply involved in the area's lumber operations. David Sword, Thomas's eldest son, inherited much of his father's expertise and followed him into the lumber camps. He spent his whole life in the bush and, well into his seventies, he was still working in the industry during the 1920s. David also inherited his father's farmstead, and built an impressive two-storey brick home called Riverdale upon the property.

David's daughter, Ella, wed Guy Smith, one of the most accomplished lumbermen in the Muskoka-Parry Sound region. His father had died young, leaving 10-year old Guy as the man of the house. He knew that the best way to earn a living in the area was by working in the timber industry and began to prepare himself for the day when he could join the lumber camps. Guy would roll a stout fence-post into a pond and, in his own words he "got to manage that cedar post so that when I started to drive the big pine, I could walk over it just the same as you walk on the road." He joined his first lumber camp at the tender age of 14, after convincing a neighbour to take him along when he left to join the Seguin drive. The youngster never looked back and became a legend in the industry.

Another of David Sword's offspring — son John and his wife Annie — decided to open a hotel where the road crossed the railway tracks. The Maple Lake Hotel was a two-storey frame building with a wide, shaded verandah, half a dozen modestly furnished rooms and a large bar. At first, its main business came from serving drinks to the men working the logging camps in the area, and consequently the bar could become quite boisterous at times. It was Annie who kept the booze-soaked men in line. Anyone who didn't meet her standards of behaviour was promptly ushered to the door.

By the late 1890s, the Maple Lake Hotel had become a favorite destination for American tourists who wanted to sample a taste of the "true northern wilds." Originally these patrons arrived on special trains known as Buffalo Flyers, but even after these were discontinued in 1905 the Americans continued to make the trip by car. When John decided to retire around 1914, the hotel was sold to his nephew, Percy Sword, who continued to operate the hotel for another decade.

Even the village general store was operated by a Sword. Originally built in 1890 by the Ludgate Lumber Company to serve the needs of the millhands and their families, around 1900 the store came into the possession of Thomas Sword, Percy's brother and David's nephew. The store was the heart of the community, a place where locals not only did all their shopping but also much of their socializing — oftentimes people would lounge upon the porch or, in foul weather, around a pot-bellied stove.

Thomas Sword died prematurely in 1921, compelling his widow, Lyde, to continue the business. Lyde Sword was a woman of principle who decided she would no longer sell tobacco in her store. The village men, predictably, were quite upset at the inconvenience and began to patronize an *ad hoc* store established by a local gentleman with no compunction about selling tobacco or any other goods. Lyde Sword quickly realized her mistake and began stocking tobacco once more.

For children, the centre of village life was the one-room schoolhouse built just south of the village in 1904. But it was far more than a school. It also served as a community centre, and because there was no dedicated church in Maple Lake Station, the building found itself playing host to religious services. The schoolhouse was a source of considerable pride for the entire community, a place belonging to no one and everyone.

The 1910s and early 1920s were a sort of gilded era in the brief history of Maple Lake Station, at which time the village boasted the store, hotel, school, blacksmith and railway station and a population of nearly 100. A stagecoach linked the village to nearby communities.

But a slow, almost imperceptible decline in fortunes had already begun. The mill, from about 1910 under the ownership of the Sheppard Lumber Company, remained in operation until the early 1920s. By this time, however, there was no longer sufficient timber left to keep the mill profitable. The saws fell silent.

The loss of the sawmill was a profound blow to the community. Lumbering had kept the farms in the area viable considerably longer than would otherwise have been the case, and when this source of supplemental income was lost most local farmers simply could not survive and were forced to move away.

Other blows were driving the community to its knees at the same time. The Maple Lake Hotel never recovered from the drought of visitors that accompanied World War I. Few tourists — American or Canadian — rediscovered the hotel even after the guns fell silent in 1918, and with the onset of prohibition in Ontario the once-raucous barroom suddenly fell eerily silent too. As a result, the Maple Lake Hotel was no longer a viable business. Owner John Sword sold the building to his nephew, Percy, then moved away.

Percy's son Jack Sword, now a 90-year-old resident of Parry Sound, was born in the hotel in 1917 and in his youth spent many years playing in the cavernous bar and among the dust-draped guest rooms. "It was a large building with many modern features for the time; my father was always very progressive," he says wistfully. "The entire building was lit with carbide gas. Not many buildings had carbide gas because it was expensive and dangerous. Gas would be piped by copper tubing from a storage tank to all rooms, creating open flames in wall-mounted lamps. There was also a telephone in the hotel, the first in the township."

In 1925 the Canadian National Railway (CN, which had bought out Booth's railway) decided to rename Maple Lake Station to avoid confusion with another stop of the same name along its line. Thereafter, both the railway facility and the village itself were known as Swords. But traffic along the route was slowing appreciably, thanks largely to the demise of the local lumber and tourism industries. From a peak of more than 20 trains per day rumbling through Swords a decade earlier, the number was by now reduced to perhaps 10 daily, often less. In 1946 CN, citing a lack of use, made the decision to close the Swords station. A decade later, the entire line was closed.

By this date, the village had atrophied to only a few scattered farms. The old general store continued to serve the dwindling population for a few more years, resisting the tides of time that would sweep away the little village. It was a fight the weathered old store could not possibly win, and by the early 1960s this final remnant of Sword's heyday had closed as well. A once-thriving and proud village had died.

And yet, some truly atmospheric relics remain. The former general store, for example, still overlooks the road. The porch upon which villagers once congregated sags under the weight of the years and the paint fades in the elements, but otherwise it remains in remarkable condition. Beside it, the former Ottawa, Arnprior & Parry Sound Railway is now a recreational trail used by hikers and snowmobilers. To the south

The store is one of the few buildings remaining in Swords, but the years have not been kind.

of the store, obscured by dense foliage, sit a former lumber company home and several dilapidated outbuildings. About half a mile farther south lies the schoolhouse, still in use as a community centre.

"The village I remember is mostly gone," says Jack Sword, a sad pall falling over his spirit. "The people are gone, the buildings gone."

While we today would consider Swords a dead community — a ghost town — it remains very much alive for Jack. He sees it all in his mind's eye as memories bring the community once again to life, restoring weathered and lost buildings to their former glory and repopulating the village with the souls of the departed. As long as Jack Sword lives, so will the community that his family founded.

Chapter 6
The McCoys

Locations: The McCoys are accessible only by boat or sea kayak. Big McCoy is ringed by dangerous shoals, so take extreme caution when approaching. Unlike the other ghost towns in this book, a visit to the McCoys in early spring or late autumn is not recommended, due to seasonal storms that make Georgian Bay all but impassable to small craft. Instead, opt for high summer.
Driving Time from Toronto: 2.5 hours.

In the nineteenth century, countless tiny fishing villages, some inhabited only seasonally, occupied the barren and windswept islands of Georgian Bay. It was a time when the bounty of the lake, in the form of whitefish and lake trout, was seemingly endless and provided a way of life for thousands of hardy mariners.

It was this industry that brought human habitation, tenuous as it might have been, to the McCoys. Located just north of Parry Sound, the McCoys are a tiny chain of islands consisting of a few small islets and a single larger island called

The McCoys

The McCoy Islands, once the seasonal home of fishermen, are isolated on the waters of Georgian Bay and have both unpredictable weather and dangerous shoals.

Big McCoy. It is a forlorn area, isolated both by the tempestuous weather of Georgian Bay and by the dangerous shoals that lurk just out of sight below the water's surface. Most of the islands are almost devoid of vegetation, and those trees that do exist are the stunted, wind-sculpted tamarack. Only Big McCoy can boast a real forest.

Big McCoy became the centre of human activity in the chain because of its size, relative wealth of resources and a sheltered cove on the western shore.

The windswept island owes its name to its first inhabitant, a disreputable man named McCoy. He came here to trade among the native people, and established a ramshackle trading post and residence on the island. He already had a long list of crimes to his name, so perhaps when he came to this isolated location he was fleeing his past. The dark-hearted McCoy was anything but a fair and honest dealer, and made a tidy profit by fleecing his native customers. Worse yet, he openly bragged to other Europeans about his underhanded dealings, daring anyone to stop him. No one did, and for years his crimes went unpunished.

It was inevitable that word of McCoy's dishonesty would get back to the native people themselves. When it did, they were enraged, and one young man took matters into his own hands. On a September evening, under the pale blue glow of a full moon, the native stepped ashore on McCoy's Island. As he made his way towards the cabin, slipping from shadow to shadow, he was fairly certain that McCoy would be asleep, but still he took no chances and proceeded with the stealth of a cat. Then he was inside the cabin and looming large over the sleeping trader like an avenging angel. He fell upon McCoy and justice was done. McCoy would cheat no more.

With the trader dead, the islands were left uninhabited for several years. It wasn't until the golden age of the Great Lakes commercial fishery in the last half of the nineteenth century that the McCoys once again supported human settlement.

The cold waters of Georgian Bay became the fishing domain of a handful of large companies, primarily the Buffalo Fish Company, the Gauthier Company, the Booth Company and the Dominion Fish Company. These companies in turn hired or contracted individual fishermen, who operated out of 26-foot skiffs, to provide them with their catch. Because the fishing grounds were far distant from most mainland ports, anchorages were established in the small harbours of islands and shoals across the length and breadth of Georgian Bay.

A community arose on Big McCoy Island. From April to October the sheltered cove was crowded with fishing skiffs, and its shores were lined with cabins, though winter found most people back in their home ports. Many fishermen brought their wives and children with them, creating a real — if only seasonal — community. In peak years, perhaps a few dozen people huddled together in the island's draughty shanties.

Residents enjoyed few amenities. Besides the crude homes, the net sheds and the icehouses where the fish were stored, there were no other buildings of note. Ringing the sheltered cove were wharves and a jetty, and it was from here that company tugs picked up the fish to transport them to freezers in Collingwood and Wiarton. Church services were held in an *ad hoc* manner, either in someone's home or in an empty cabin presided over by a layman. Provisions came from a floating general store that made periodic visits.

As a result, even more so than most, this community had to be self-sufficient. Everyone on the island had a small shed where they kept chickens for fresh eggs and goats for milk. Many residents also brought along pigs that would be fed on cull fish. "We'd boil them [the fish] in a big iron kettle, heads and all, and you want to see the pigs eat them," remembered Jim Parr, a long-time Georgian Bay fisherman intimately familiar with the lake. "About a month before you killed them you had to stop feeding them fish, we fed them mash so they wouldn't taste so fishy."

The life of a fisherman was taxing. Oftentimes the 26-foot skiffs would put out at six o'clock in the morning and would not return again until one or two the next morning. The men would sleep for a few hours, without taking their clothes off or washing, then wake again at four or five to prepare their nets for a new day. This routine would continue for months on end, with only Sunday set aside as a day for rest.

Fatigue made the already dangerous job even more hazardous. Most fishermen couldn't swim, so a misstep aboard the boat could end in disaster, and more than one man became entangled in nets and drowned. Lurking shoals that could hole a boat were always a threat, and the fierce storms for which Georgian Bay is known could materialize in minutes to swamp or overturn a vessel or drive it onto the rocks.

This unique lifestyle didn't endure long. By the early years of the twentieth century Georgian Bay could no longer sustain a large-scale commercial fishery, as fish stocks had been depleted by overfishing and their spawning grounds fouled by sawdust. Those fishermen who remained began turning to larger, gas-powered boats that could reach the fishing grounds directly from mainland ports. As a result, the seasonal fishing villages that dotted Georgian Bay's islands became obsolete and began to disappear.

The fishing hamlet on Big McCoy, never large to begin with, fell prey to these changing dynamics faster than most of its contemporaries and was already shrinking by the turn of the century. By the 1920s it was almost completely abandoned, though some fishermen continued to use the island as a base for their operations on occasion. Probably the last individual to make use of the island as a fishing post was a man named Stalker who, according to Jim Parr, "had a steam tug and fished pound nets" here in the 1940s.

Owing to their remoteness the McCoys have been undisturbed by development or vandalism. While most of the shanties have long since been battered into ruin by the winds blowing off Lake Huron, reminders of the fishing operation are very much in evidence. A few sagging cabins still exist, leaning more and more with each passing season. There are also pins in the rocks where the sailboats used to tie up, piles of wood indicating the location of former cabins and — if one looks hard enough — a wealth of relics both among the rocks and in the waters just offshore.

On the island's eastern side, far away from the former anchorage, there is a perfect mound of rocks measuring 35 by 60 feet. There's some debate about the origins of this oddity, but most agree that it is probably an ancient native burial ground. Either way, it offers an atmospheric find to close out an afternoon of exploration.

Lying far out in the cold, dark waters of Georgian Bay, the McCoy Islands are home to one of the most isolated and forlorn ghost towns to be found anywhere in Ontario. It is hard to imagine a less likely place for human habitation, and if it were not for the bounty of the lake the islands never would have been settled. In the late nineteenth century, two million pounds of whitefish and trout were caught each year, but when that bounty inevitably ran out, the fishermen quickly raised sail and turned their backs on the barren islands. When they did, the small settlement that had clung to the windswept rocks for nearly half a century was quickly forgotten.

The Spectre of Big McCoy

Big McCoy is a picturesque island known for its rugged terrain. Yet, many people who make the lengthy trip to the isolated rock are more than eager to leave. They have seen, or more often heard, the frightening spectre of Big McCoy.

The tale behind the haunting is part legend and part history. It became common knowledge among those who sailed near the McCoys that the disreputable man for whom the islands were named appeared regularly on the jagged shores.

It's said that during every full moon in September since his murder at the hands of an enraged Indian whom he had cheated, the ghost of the dead McCoy begins pacing the island. He becomes more active and agitated under the full moon, however, when his mournful howls escape from the depths of the island's woods and echo out across the waters of Georgian Bay. Hearing McCoy's cries, as he mourns his own death and curses his killers, is a spine-chilling experience, one that leaves some people so frightened that they vow never to return to the accursed place.

Bill Sing, a Parry Sound fisherman, was one such man. After a lifetime spent facing the dangers of the Bay, there was little that truly scared Bill. He had endured groundings on hidden shoals, sudden storms and near-drowning with grim determination, but he always returned after every brush with death to the waters of Georgian Bay. Yet he was so frightened after only a few hours on Big McCoy that he refused to ever again set foot on the island. What had he encountered that could possibly scar him so?

It was back in the early years of the twentieth century that Bill was forced to seek safe anchorage at Big McCoy Island to ride out a nasty storm buffeting the bay. The combination of gale-force winds, white-capped waves and pelting rain that reduced visibility to zero made remaining out on the waters virtual suicide. The fisherman was stranded on an uninhabited, haunted and completely isolated island.

Exhausted from his ordeal, Bill staggered into one of the abandoned cabins and fell asleep. His deep slumber was interrupted by a wretched scream. He was awake and alert as quickly as if cold water had been poured over him, and he felt cold rivulets of fear trickling over his skin. Moments later, there was a second wail. Terrified, the fisherman raced to his boat and immediately cast off, paying no heed to the storm that was still raging unabated. For him to risk death by braving the Bay rather than spend another moment on the island says much about his frame of mind. He had, quite literally, been scared witless.

Bill Sing was true to his word, and never returned to the site of his terrifying ordeal.

Others have had similar frightening experiences. In recent years, the islands have become a popular destination with sea kayakers, many of whom camp overnight to enjoy the solitude. Some have come to regret the decision to stop over.

"My friends and I — there were six of us in total — decided to paddle out to Big McCoy and spend a few nights there. During the day we would explore the smaller islands," says Kelli, a young woman experienced in both the outdoors and sea kayaking on Georgian Bay. "We had tried the trip once before, but bad weather prevented us from launching. Maybe that was Fate trying to tell us something."

Kelli researches all of her destinations and she admits to being aware of the history and folklore surrounding the islands, but she never put much stock in the ghost story. Until the first night on Big McCoy.

"For years strange, unexplained happenings have been witnessed by boaters near the island," she says. "We talked about them around the campfire, trying to spook each other out. Maybe we put ourselves on edge, because by the time we went to bed I was uneasy."

The hours passed slowly and fitfully. Sleep did not come easily. Every time she closed her eyes, Kelli's imagination would take over and every sound became a vengeance-seeking ghost. She was staring at the fire when suddenly she heard a hoarse whisper from behind her. The words were unintelligible, but the tone sounded angry, frightening. She quickly rolled over to see piercing eyes that gleamed from the woods, making her shudder.

"I screamed and immediately everyone was awake. The eyes flickered and were gone; no one else saw them. But that was just the beginning of the torment. We saw strange lights in the woods, like a lantern or flashlight bobbing up and down, but they flickered on and off randomly. And there was a general feeling of unease that couldn't be placed, but we all felt it."

Kelli and her friends left the next morning, and like Bill Sing before them, have never returned to the McCoy Islands.

It seems that while the native who killed McCoy prevented the unscrupulous trader from cheating any more customers, the killing could not erase the man's blight from the land. Indeed, his murder did not just stain the rocks of McCoy Island with blood, but also with evil energies that exist to this day.

Chapter 7
Eugenia Falls

Location: Eugenia is located northwest of Toronto. Take Highway 10 to Flesherton, turning right at the lights onto Regional Road 4. Turn left onto County Road 13 (Beaver Valley Road). Eugenia is 3 km along the road.
Driving Time from Toronto: 1.5 hours.

Gold! In the nineteenth century the very utterance of the word turned practical men into dreamers. With a little luck and some hard work even the poorest person had a shot at unimaginable riches. Like Tombstone and Deadwood in the American West, Eugenia Falls was originally a boomtown founded on the simple principle of "get rich quick." But unlike its notorious American counterparts, which lost their fortunes as soon as the ore was gone, Eugenia Falls actually experienced greater prosperity when the boom had faded.

The sun was setting on a hot summer's day in 1854 when Sandy Brownlea and a friend, hunting in the rugged forests north of Shelburne, heard a distant roar echoing through the trees. Spellbound, the two men trudged towards the sound, determined to find its source.

With each step the thunder grew stronger, until finally

In the 19th century, the power of Eugenia Falls was harnessed to run mills that lined the waterway, and the village prospered.

the forest drew apart to reveal a waterfall crashing 210 feet down a sheer rock face.

The men were transfixed by the sight and stood in awe of the mighty waterfall for many minutes. Finally, they began to inch their way down the steep-sided gorge into the narrow canyon below. While exploring the gorge, Brownlea noticed how some of the rocks seemed to sparkle as the setting sun caught them in its rays. Looking closer, the men became convinced that these rocks were laced with gold. Hearts threatened to burst from their chests as the fast friends pondered the possibility of riches beyond their wildest dreams.

Filled with excitement, the men returned home. Somehow, word of their discovery soon leaked out. One story suggests that Brownlea let it slip while enjoying a drink with some friends at a tavern. Slightly inebriated, he began to boast of his find and soon enough the riches of Eugenia Falls became common knowledge.

Instantly, gold fever swept the area, and more than 200 gold seekers swarmed the boulder-strewn gully, hoping to emulate the success of the California Gold Rush of 1849. The area was littered with tents and shanties, some of which housed primitive taverns or stores established by enterprising individuals. So it was that the community of Eugenia Falls sprang up practically overnight, turning the area that so recently had been wilderness into a hive of activity.

An 800-acre townsite was surveyed for the growth that everyone expected. The Crimean War, which saw Britain and France allied against Russia, was at its height and patriotic fervour was running high. As a result, the gridlike streets all bore the names of battles or principal characters in the conflict, including Alma, Balaclava, Raglan, Codrington and Pelletier. Indeed, the community itself was named to reflect the war then playing on everyone's mind: Eugenia Falls honours Princess Eugenia, the consort of French Emperor Napoleon II, an ally-in-arms of the British Empire.

With its regal name and large townsite, most people expected Eugenia Falls to transform into a new metropolis.

Then one day someone decided to have the "gold" assayed. To everyone's shock and disappointment, it turned out to be nothing more than iron pyrites — fool's gold — a completely worthless ore. Instantly, Eugenia Falls' glitter had tarnished, and the frenzied gold rush faded as quickly as it had begun. The tents disappeared and the ramshackle cabins were abandoned to the elements.

For a few years nobody took any further interest in Eugenia Falls. That changed in 1859, when William and Robert Purdy arrived and stood on the lip of the ravine. The prospectors who had fled after the gold rush faded had been too shortsighted to see the true riches that the site offered, but the Purdy brothers were men of vision. To their ambitious spirits, the cascading river and the crashing falls whispered of opportunity. They recognized that Eugenia Falls was an ideal location to supply power for mills, a far more reliable means of getting rich in nineteenth-century Ontario than prospecting for gold. A steady flow of water meant great potential for profit — and profit was the prime tenet of the Purdy brothers' religion.

Later that year, they built a sawmill along the Beaver River at the top of the falls, and in 1860 they added a gristmill as well. William Purdy was the more ambitious of the siblings. By 1865 he also owned a combined general store and post office that was decorated with giant moose antlers and samples of Eugenia Falls' notorious fool's gold. Later, he built a tavern to complete his local business empire. William

Purdy was undoubtedly the richest and most important man in town, and solidified his authority by being named Justice of the Peace.

Eugenia Falls grew rapidly, with its mills and townsite stretching at least half a mile along the banks of the Beaver River. With an estimated population of 200 by 1865, the community quickly developed most of the amenities a small town needs, laid out in the formal gridlike pattern established earlier.

S. T. Halsted (later John Somers) operated the Eugenia Hotel, John Duncan added a second store, and there were blacksmiths, coopers, shoemakers and carpenters' shops. Other industries followed the Purdy's lead and flocked to the site, turning the bustling ravine-side village into a manufacturing power in the township. T. W. Wilson ran a prosperous carriage factory and planing mill, while American-born carpenter J. B. Sloan built a sash, door and chair factory.

As with most settlers in nineteenth-century Ontario, those at Eugenia Falls were by and large God-fearing folk intent upon providing their children with religious guidance and formal education. As a result, as soon as the village was established, its citizens came together in order to build two churches, one Methodist and the other Presbyterian, and a one-room school.

The village thrived for three decades, with the population soaring to more than 300. Eugenia Falls seemed to have a glorious future.

Eugenia Falls

The heady optimism of its citizens was only reinforced when William Hogg, a wealthy industrialist from Hogg's Hollow in Toronto, took note of the waterfall in 1895. It was the dawn of the age of electricity and all across the province primitive hydroelectric plants were being built to provide local communities with lighting and industrial power. Hogg wanted to harness the power of Eugenia Falls. If his venture proved successful, there would undoubtedly be economic advantages to the community itself, and so most residents were enthusiastic.

Hogg built a facility capable of producing 70 kilowatts of electricity, enough to provide lights for both Eugenia Falls and nearby Flesherton, as well as to power at least one local chopping mill. Hogg was pleased with his success, and was sure he could build upon it. Unfortunately, he died in 1900 before he could secure additional interest or investment in his plant.

Although Hogg's endeavour can only be considered a modest success, it had demonstrated the potential of the falls for hydroelectric power. Taking up the deceased visionary's mantle, a group of investors called the Georgian Bay Power Company (GBPC) arrived in 1907 with a much more ambitious scheme to profit from Eugenia Falls. After purchasing the land and all power rights above and below the falls, the GBPC carved an 860-foot turbine tunnel through the rock from the top of the falls to its base. The turbine tunnel would better harness the water's flow, in theory greatly improving upon the output of Hogg's power plant. At each entrance of the shaft an imposing stone arch was erected.

We'll never know if this enterprise would have been more fruitful than its predecessor. Its construction proved so expensive that it bankrupted the investors who, without recourse, abandoned the plant and gave up on the scheme. Despite the obvious power contained within the river, two successive attempts to harness it had failed in the sense that it left Hogg bankrupt and was never more than a small-scale industry. Finally, in 1913, the Beaver River was tamed, although not at the falls themselves. In that year Ontario's Hydro-Electric Power Commission dammed Eugenia Lake, well upstream from the falls, and built a pair of mile-long pipes to a power plant in the Beaver Valley. At long last, Hogg's dream had been realized and Eugenia Falls — or at least the river that feeds it — was producing electricity on a scale worthy of note.

By this date, however, the fortunes of Eugenia Falls were in the midst of a steep and seemingly irrecoverable dive. While the power brokers came, the railways did not, choosing instead to run tracks through nearby Flesherton. This slight undermined Eugenia Falls' industries, relegating it to second-tier status. Over the ensuing decades Flesherton grew at Eugenia Falls' expense, taking over its position as largest and most prosperous town in the region, and siphoning away businesses and citizens.

Eugenia Falls, however, proved a stubborn little community. It refused to die completely, even though it teetered precariously on the brink for many decades. It still exists today as a tiny collection of homes and businesses, barely recognizable as a distinct community and certainly never hinting at its boomtown past. The buoyant Eugenia Falls of the late 1800s has disappeared completely, never to return.

And yet, if you look hard enough, you can find enough relics of the past to suggest that something extraordinary occurred here in the distant past.

Several decaying, crumbling buildings, and even one that is partially burned-out, straddle Pelletier Street, the village's former main thoroughfare, as it leads into Eugenia Falls Conservation Area. Among these forlorn structures is the former general store, which stands out from the rest by both its relative grandeur and its careful upkeep. Though no longer a mercantile, it is still inhabited and serves as one of the more poignant reminders that this wearied community did indeed experience a golden age, a long time ago.

The former hotel, distinctive for its size and second-storey balcony, is another atmospheric throwback to Eugenia Falls' nineteenth-century heyday. If these walls could only talk, the colourful, alcohol-enhanced stories they would tell would surely fill an entire book. Sadly, most of these tales are lost forever now.

For the most intriguing ruins, visitors must delve into the wooded confines of the conservation area. The most obvious is the graffiti-laden powerhouse from the early attempts to harness the falls. It is not a particularly impressive building — just four squat brick walls, not much bigger in size than many modern living rooms — but somehow it is reflective of the industriousness upon which Eugenia Falls placed its hopes.

Across the river, hidden for most of the year by dense foliage, lies the stone archway that marks the upper entrance of the turbine tunnel. The tunnel has long since been filled in for safety reasons, but the archaic-looking stone arches are fascinating nonetheless.

Finally, after a short walk upstream, you'll come across some planks in the riverbed and within its shallows. These mark the site of Purdy's sawmill. They provide the only evidence, fragmentary though it may be, of the operation that propelled Purdy to prominence.

But of course, the main attraction of the location, then as now, is the majestic Eugenia Falls themselves. They capture the imagination as surely as they must have captured Sandy Brownlea's when he initially discovered the falls 150 years ago. It is not hard to see why the early settlers believed that this magical setting was fated for something special.

Ghost at Eugenia Falls

Eugenia Falls must surely have been admired by native people well before Europeans stumbled upon their majesty in 1852. Yet, despite the obvious beauty of the location, the local natives avoided it. It was a place of rumour and fear. Where the shadows of the falls stretch, tragedy follows. Wandering the terrain was a ghostly young woman, the murdered victim of jealous rage, who served as a frightening harbinger of doom.

Supposedly, the body of the young woman was never recovered, and instead was allowed to slowly rot upon the rocks. The ravine became her tomb.

The exact date of the tragic series of events and the names of the participants have been forgotten with the passage of the centuries. There were three principals in this tragic tale: the lovely young native woman, her adoring secret lover and her vengeful husband.

The story begins the day the husband discovered his wife's secret. His heart trembled. He felt an overwhelming sense of betrayal and loss, never for a moment considering how his callous neglect had driven his wife into the arms of another. How could he have been so blind? Why hadn't he noticed before?

Something in his mind snapped and he became fixed on one single purpose: revenge. The angry husband slunk back to the village and awaited the return of his wife from a passionate liaison. She arrived home and did her best to mask the glow that always shone from her heart and in her smile after being in her lover's embrace. Now that her husband knew of her secret, it only fuelled the fires of hatred burning him. But he was patient. He wanted to savour his revenge.

Later that night he convinced her to take a walk with

him in the woods. She didn't suspect a thing as they weaved their way hand-in-hand through the dark forest. The danger didn't even dawn on her when they arrived at the lip of the waterfall, the very scene of so many of her discreet meetings. In the darkness she neither saw the evil glint in her husband's eye, nor the cold smile that suddenly stretched across his face. She couldn't know that he delighted in the irony that the place where she felt most alive would be the place of her death.

Only when strong arms gripped her shoulders and dragged her to the edge of the precipice did she finally realize the fate that awaited her. She struggled, but her husband's bearlike arms were strengthened by war and hunting, and her flailing was in vain. She screamed in terror as she was thrown from the cliff. Her screams were still echoing through the ravine when her body crashed upon the rocks below.

On certain days, the echoes of this crime are still heard today.

In the years since her death, native and European people alike have heard the terrible wails of the murdered young woman echoing through the ravine. Sometimes, it begins atop the falls and disappears into the abyss below, as if her spirit is forced to relive her final, terrifying moments. It is also said that the evil essence of her dark-hearted killer remains forever trapped within the waters below the falls. It's a purgatory from which he cannot escape. His spirit seeks vengeance upon mankind, believing that our judgment of his crime prevents him from enjoying the respite of a peaceful afterlife. When people venture down to the river and walk upon the rocks, it is said that the ghost will literally rise up from the water to grab hold of them, drag them into river and claim them as his victims.

The spiteful ghost is said to be a horror to behold. Accounts suggest that he is little more than a dark shadow, bulbous and uneven, with long groping arms. The only thing that hints at his former existence as a human being are his dead white eyes, which blaze intensely with hatred for all mortals — but most particularly for women.

A truly frightening account of the ghost at Eugenia Falls was posted by an anonymous teenaged girl on the website of the Toronto & Ontario Ghosts and Hauntings Research Society. It demonstrates that something evil lurks behind the veil of beauty at this enchanting locale.

The girl, then much younger, was with her best friend when the story begins. They visited the falls one glorious summer's day and were "wandering around, acting like kids." Their explorations brought them to a brick wall that lines the top of the gorge and prevents people from falling to the rocks 130 feet below. The girls leaned over the wall, marvelling at the sheer drop and the rugged beauty of the boulder-strewn ravine. It dawned on them that the view of the waterfall from down below would be spectacular. Intent on seeing the falls in all their glory, they resolved to make their way down.

It was an ill-considered decision that nearly proved fatal.

The two girls walked, slid and climbed down an uneven path that led at length to the base of the ravine. Here they could cross the river or make their way upstream by leaping from one algae-covered rock to another. "The water level was a bit higher because it was just the beginning of summer, and we weren't sure we wanted to cross or not," explains the girl. "While we were standing we felt darkness come down on us regardless of the fact that it was bright and sunny. All the birds or animals fell silent…. A few seconds after that we heard a cry for help by a young woman. Then something grabbed my ankle and tried to pull me towards the water, like it wanted to kill me."

In desperation, the girl yanked her foot away from her invisible assailant, freeing herself from his grip. She screamed in fright, ordering her friend to run. Together, they raced back up the path they had only moments before descended, their hearts thumping in their chests from fear and exertion.

"We felt we were being chased by this thing and I believe I saw it, but I'm not positive," the girl continues. "As soon as we got to the highway, it was gone. Just like that. I was told that the cry for help was actually an Indian girl that had been thrown over the falls long ago, and the thing that grabbed my ankle was her murderer."

Like most people who have had run-ins with the supernatural, she has never really gotten over the experience. "Now that I'm 15, I can still feel the hand on my ankle, like it left something there forever." Perhaps the ghost left a permanent wound on the young girl's emotions. Many believe the icy touch of the undead leaves scars that simply do not heal with the passage of time.

Though few visitors encounter the vengeful wraith, most people who visit Eugenia Falls are permanently affected by the experience. It's so beautiful that there's enough scenery to fill an entire roll of film. And yet, part of the allure is the unmistakable aura of danger that surrounds the falls. The rocks below are ragged and threatening, and during peak seasons the water crashes down upon them with untamed power. You can't help but be impressed by the sight of the rugged canyon running off to your left like a jagged knife wound cut into the earth.

In a primal environment such as this, it's not hard to imagine a bloodthirsty spirit lurking out of sight for the unwary to stumble into its grip. At least one person, a beautiful native woman, fell victim to evil here. Who knows how many other corpses have joined hers at the bottom of Eugenia Falls?

Chapter 8
Kerr Lake

Location: Kerr Lake lies only a few kilometres east of Cobalt, and is one of more than a dozen highlights on the still-developing Silver Trail. Cobalt is about 110 km north of North Bay, a short distance east of Highway 11 along Highway 118. Maps of this driving route are available at The Bunker Military Museum and at Cobalt's Northern Ontario Mining Museum. Both of these attractions are, incidentally, well worth a visit.
Driving Time from Toronto: 5.5 hours.

Cobalt is far removed from the headlines today, but in 1906 the town appeared prominently in newspapers all across the world. Its rich silver deposits were among the largest anywhere yet found.

A silver rush of unprecedented proportions followed this discovery, giving rise to the town of Cobalt seemingly overnight. Initially, settlement and development was centred exclusively upon the townsite and the initial silver vein, but in the coming years prospectors spread out into the surrounding wilderness in search of new, untapped veins. Smaller communities — mining camps with few of the luxuries of life afforded by teeming Cobalt — soon appeared among the trees and rocks.

One of the larger camps was Kerr Lake, a haphazard community huddled upon the shores of the body of water for which it was named.

The first prospectors arrived at Kerr Lake in 1904 to find veins of silver as wide as sidewalks running deep into the earth. Individual prospectors could not possibly hope to extract the silver on their own, so it was inevitable that large mining consortiums would acquire these valuable claims. Soon the landscape was dotted with head frames, mills for crushing stone and other industrial buildings.

There were a dozen mines in the area, but the largest producers were the Crown Reserve Mine, the Foster Cobalt Mine and the Kerr Lake Mine. Kerr Lake Mine boasted the lowest production costs of any mine in Canada, and from 1904 to 1922 extracted 27 million ounces of silver — worth more than $500 million in contemporary currency, or about $10 billion today.

While a maze of mine shafts was being dug into the rock around the lake, surveyors began to realize that a potential untapped bonanza existed *under* the lake. With this in mind, in 1906 the Crown Reserve Mine purchased from the Ontario Government the mining rights to all 23 acres lying under the lake for $178,000 and yearly royalties. Buying the rights was easy; exploiting them was something else entirely.

The mining camp at Kerr Lake was one of the most prosperous in the Cobalt area. Today, skeletal headframes and decaying camp buildings are eerie remains.

To extract the silver, Kerr Lake would have to be drained. The first primitive effort occurred in 1907, when the lake was lowered 8 feet by means of a ditch leading west to Glen Lake. This provided a site to sink the main shaft to a depth of 300 feet.

In 1913, a pumping operation was begun to drain the lake in its entirety. A total of 600 million gallons of water and silt were removed. The lake refilled naturally every winter, and so the time-consuming process of pumping it dry would have to be repeated on an annual basis. Once the lake was dry, miners could return to the trenches and shafts they had dug the year before. Unfortunately, as the lake was drained fish would seek refuge in these depths and, when the last of the water was removed, they would die there. The stench of rotting fish was so rancid during the hot summer months that it would overwhelm many miners. Nevertheless, the process was worthwhile. Between 1908 and 1921, the Crown Reserve Mine produced more than 20 million ounces of silver from the lakebed and the shafts bored 800 feet below.

But while the mine owners undeniably made their fortunes, life for the miners was harrowing, unhealthy, uncertain and unprofitable. They operated in a half-lit world, toiling on the edge of life and death. They appeared to one another in the gloom as little more than shadows, which was perhaps appropriate in that one never knew when an accident might claim his partner. It was expected — and considered acceptable — that a man would be lost every year in each shaft. If a miner did not die from an accidental cave-in, exploding gas pocket or flooding upon inadvertently drilling into an underwater lake or stream, illness was sure to eventually catch up to him in old age. Many were crippled with arthritis or rheumatism, wracked by dry cough brought upon by "black lung" or felled by lung cancer.

To make matters worse, the miners were paid but a pittance. And there was little in the way of job security — every ton of ore taken from the ground brought even the greatest mine one ton closer to depletion. But they held to the belief that the hard rock of the Canadian Shield would always provide for them, that if one vein wound down a new one would be found and exploited.

What kind of man would accept such risks? By and large, the miners of Kerr Lake were poor and uneducated individuals who had only recently immigrated to North America from foreign nations. The place was a melting pot, with men primarily drawn from eastern Europe, the British Isles and Finland, with a smattering of Italians and native-born Canadians stirred into the mix. For many, toiling in the mines of Northern Ontario was the only work they could find.

But it wasn't just men who lived and worked in this rough mining camp. There were women as well, though proper society would hardly have considered them ladies. Most were prostitutes, serving both the men of Kerr Lake and nearby Cobalt, where brothels had been outlawed. At least two dens of ill repute operated in the camp, providing any form of female companionship if the price was right. Few women fell into the trade willingly. Most ladies of the night were formerly respectable wives who had lost their mates to the mines and were forced to accept the only employment then available for women in the area. The silver boom was a crapshoot, and these unfortunate women were the losers in a high-risk game.

For the miners, death could strike suddenly and without warning, so they needed an unshakeable faith in a higher being and some divine purpose in order to return to the mines on a daily basis. It was too horrifying to even consider that one's life could be taken away by something as random as a mining accident. Such strong convictions were especially needed at Kerr Lake, where the Crown Reserve Mine had by far the highest death rate in the whole Cobalt Camp — 28 per cent of men who entered the gloomy depths would eventually not resurface.

The single greatest loss of life occurred in 1907, when Cobalt and the surrounding camps were beset by a smallpox epidemic brought on by poor sanitation. "Men died so rapidly," recalled Elizabeth MacEwan, "that each morning showed the dead along the roadside awaiting removal." Temporary hospitals, known as pesthouses, were set up away from the communities, but doctors — fearful of spreading the sickness — left the disease-ravaged victims to fend for themselves. One of the few physicians to continue caring for the ill was Kerr Lake resident William Drummond, a former doctor who by then had given up his practice to run the Drummond Mine.

Unlike most of the mine owners, who cared not a whit for the men who worked in their name, Drummond risked his own welfare to care for the sick and dying. He was tireless in his vigil, working beyond endurance to nurse patients back to health or at least make them comfortable in their final days. In the end, it cost him dearly. The selflessness Dr. Drummond demonstrated during the outbreak shattered his own health, and he died a few months later in his home at Kerr Lake. A memorial cairn was placed on the ruins of his chimney in 1935, but has long since been removed to Cobalt's town square where it can be better appreciated.

In light of all the hazards associated with their occupation, miners clearly needed a place to pray and, too often, a place to conduct services for fallen comrades. In the summer of 1911, with financial backing from the owners of the Crown Reserve Mine, the entire community came together to build a church. Despite the rugged character of the camp itself, St. Hilliard's Church was a majestic sight, a large whitewashed board-and-batten structure, its tall spire reaching up into the heavens. St. Hilliard's was the only church in the community and served all denominations equally.

The church was a respectful homage to God, yet a few short years after its construction locals must have been left wondering if somehow they had displeased the Lord. The morning of Good Friday, 1913, dawned with ominous clouds looming over the small community. Trees began to bend and sway under the relentless assault of steadily growing winds. Soon, shingles were being peeled off cabins and the camp was buffeted by blinding sheets of dirt so strong that the grit would scratch exposed skin. Walking against the wind was fruitless, and merely standing upright took all of one's strength.

It was one of the fiercest windstorms the region had ever seen, and it left a trail of destruction in its wake. One of the casualties was St. Hilliard's Church, which had been completely levelled. In the rush to build, shoddy workmanship and substandard materials had been used, with tragic results. In typically tight-fisted fashion, the mine owners refused to invest in the community from their own pockets and so St. Hilliard's was never rebuilt. Henceforth, Kerr Lake continued without the benefit of a place of worship.

Despite this setback, the community continued to grow. By 1915, there were 300 people huddled into some 40 homes, laid out in unplanned fashion between the head frames and along the web of roads that cut through the wilderness around Kerr Lake. The camp may have been multicultural in composition, and miners may have thought of one another as a brotherhood as soon as they ventured into the depths, but nonetheless they tended to congregate along ethnic lines. One small cluster of about eight homes located on the eastern side of Kerr Lake was known as Finntown, while to the southeast stood Swedetown and to the southwest Frenchtown.

Numerous businesses served the community as a whole. Among them were Joe Edward's store (later the Edwards General Store), Leonard Kirkham's billiard room, Goulet's pool room and Blanchard's store. A public school opened in 1908 to educate the offspring of miners, and there was a post office and telegraph office to keep the community in touch with the outside world.

A six-mile spur line of the Temiskaming and Northern

Ontario Railway ran to the southern end of Kerr Lake, where a freight room, station and wyes were constructed. In 1915, the line was electrified and the Nipissing Central Railway Company began running electric trolleys from Kerr Lake through Cobalt, North Cobalt, Haileybury and New Liskeard.

Kerr Lake was on the move. Clearly it was destined for even greater things. Or so people thought at the time. Instead, it became ghost town. Why? What had gone wrong?

For nearly 15 years, silver worth millions of dollars annually (or tens of millions today) was extracted from the rock around and under Kerr Lake, making mine owners extremely wealthy and providing the impetus for the development of a thriving community. But by the early 1920s, the silver was beginning to run out. Eventually, this is the reality for any mining community. That is why the camp at Kerr Lake had never really been built to last. There were no brick homes or businesses, no paved streets and no attempt at developing a sustainable infrastructure. From the start everyone realized that at some undetermined point in the future, perhaps a decade or two, perhaps a bit longer, the silver would run out and the miners would leave in search of new veins to exploit.

Kerr Lake took longer to perish than most would have predicted, however. Even as their annual returns dwindled throughout the 1920s, most of the large mines remained until almost the end of the decade. But by 1929, most of the mines had closed down, and only a sparse population of 80 was left behind. These diehards continued to produce small amounts of silver — not enough to please shareholders in London and New York, but certainly enough to provide for their own families. The school closed in 1938, by which time all of the businesses had also been boarded up.

The population continued to shrink with each passing year, but just when it seemed Kerr Lake was about to be pulled off life support and allowed to die in peace, its fortunes briefly revived. During the late 1940s, industry began to recognize that cobalt, an ore that accompanies silver but which up until now had been considered worthless, had valuable manufacturing applications. As a result, miners returned to the Kerr Lake area, digging for cobalt and silver remnants. In 1956 there were 86 people in the area, breathing renewed life into the dying community.

But the revival was short-lived. By 1960, the population of prospectors had been halved, and within the span of another decade the miners had left once more, leaving only empty shells in their wake. This time, there would be no resurrection for the mining camp.

Today, not much remains of this at-one-time vibrant mining community. But if you take the time to walk the area, you'll be pleasantly surprised with what you might find. You'll discover, for example, hidden behind the overgrown trees and shrubs, a lonely miner's cabin from long ago. Its roof has collapsed around the walls, leaving a staircase that now climbs to a nonexistent second floor. In a few years' time it is likely that the frame will finally collapse. Nevertheless, the cabin provides a reminder of a way of life in a dramatic time that's almost forgotten.

Most buildings in the ramshackle mining community were made of wood, and as a result few remain standing. The former electrical station, which provided power for both the mining operations and the supporting community, is the sole exception. All of the head-frames, ore mills and mining facilities have long since disappeared, though skeletal foundations remain.

Kerr Lake has refilled to its natural level. Along the water's edge of the lake an assortment of machinery that once worked nonstop now sits eerily and permanently silent, allowing the weather to slowly end its tired existence. The rusting and useless hulks are now monstrous monuments to the industriousness of man.

We have no frame of reference by which we can sympathize with the hardships and tragedies that the early nineteenth-century miners endured, no way of truly understanding what made them return to the nightmarish realm of the mine day after day, year after year. But these impressive remains — ruins, machinery and old trenches — that can still be seen today, provide us with a brief glimpse into their lives.

One would guess that hope kept them going, for in the back of their minds everyone secretly dreams of going from rags to riches. Sadly, in the end hope was all the reward most miners would ever have.

Kerr Lake Ghost

The days of the silver rush are long over and wilderness has slowly reclaimed the mines, and yet people visiting the location today may find that there are leftover spirits whose emotional wounds have yet to heal. This is the story of one such spirit.

A young miner who lived in Kerr Lake got a young girl pregnant. Barely more than a child himself, the miner didn't want the responsibilities of being a husband and father at this stage of his life. But he also knew the alternative would be scandalous if he didn't make things right by this young girl by marrying her and claiming the child as his own. When it came to idle gossip, the mining camp of Kerr Lake was no different from any other small community. Even in a rough mining community, there were rules to be followed, values to be upheld and responsibilities that one must accept.

It was quite a dilemma, and the miner saw no way out. He knew what society demanded that he do and against his better judgment he made the young woman his wife. The community was none the wiser. To them, the union was simply that of another young couple in love. They neither had any idea about the unborn child, nor about the inner turmoil that the miner was enduring.

The miner tried to settle into the role of husband and father-to-be, but he found it terribly confining and with each passing day his restlessness grew. He felt trapped.

In 1907, a smallpox epidemic broke out in the camp.

The dreaded disease claimed numerous victims that year, leaving gaping holes in the community. Families were torn apart by the "pox." Women were widowed and forced to provide for their young ones; husbands grieved alongside their children as wives and mothers slipped away; but it was the young who suffered the most, as they were too weak to fend off the illness. Panic struck the community. People began to lock their doors and pray that the horror of this disease would not invade their homes.

In this environment of fear and uncertainty, when most people felt only despair, the young miner suddenly felt alive with hope. He was thankful for the disease and welcomed the outbreak, silently praying that it would strike his woman down and eliminate her and the complications she brought to his life. Smallpox might free him from his prison of misery.

The young wife did fall prey to the dreaded disease. Soon she had broken out in sweats and was covered in painful red boils; it was as if her body had caught on fire and was being consumed by flames from within.

What seemed like a lifetime for the poor soul was really only a matter of days as she lingered in a nightmarish realm, mumbling incoherently most of the time for someone to relieve her of the agony she endured. The miner did nothing to ease the horrible suffering of his wife. He did not cool her fever-ravaged body with a damp cloth, nor did he answer her feeble pleas for water during her few lucid moments. He only watched and hoped that death would soon come.

The young girl, it seems, was made of stern stuff. With a strong will to see her child born, she clung desperately to life. Miraculously, her health took a turn for the better, leaving the black-hearted miner astonished that someone so close to death's door could have made such a recovery. Disappointment and anger set in as the days went by and the young mother-to-be seemed on the verge of regaining her health. The miner began to realize that smallpox would not be the answer to his problems after all.

He would now have to take matters into his own hands. Late one night, with evil clouding his judgment, the miner knelt at his wife's beside and callously whispered his love into her ear, while all he saw was a burden to be eliminated. He reached for a pillow and placed it over her face. The frail young woman tried hard to fight back. Her body convulsed as she struggled to get out from under him. Her lips desperately tried to cry for help, but her cries would go unanswered. Too weak from her fight with smallpox, she had no strength left. Sadness flooded over her as she thought of her unborn child and their tragic fate. She inhaled her last breath and it was all over. Two innocent lives were extinguished, one before it had even begun.

The miner's job was only half complete, however. With no time to waste, he gathered the body in a blanket and slipped quietly out into the darkness. He carried his burden into the woods until the deep chasm of an abandoned mine shaft lay before him. Without the slightest glimmer of remorse, the heartless man tossed his wife's body into the pit.

As her corpse disappeared into the endless darkness so too, the miner believed, did his problems.

Returning home, the murderer slipped into the role of grieving husband, simply telling the neighbours, with feigned grief and tears, that his wife had succumbed to the disease. With people dropping dead on a daily basis, no one questioned his sincerity. At least not right away.

Soon, however, it became apparent that the young woman's soul was not at rest. People began whispering that they had seen a misty woman wandering about at night, and others were sure that they had heard terrifying shrieks coming from the woods. Some even claim that the ear-piercing wails originated from deep inside the ground, echoing from a long-abandoned mine shaft.

Who knows how many other ghosts lay trapped within the long played-out mines or remain tied to the vanished community? Kerr Lake saw as much death as it did good fortune, so perhaps many broken souls linger in an eternal search for prosperity.

So if during an exploration of the ruins of Kerr Lake's once impressive mining operation you happen to hear a cry playing upon the breeze, take note. It might not be a coyote or wolf, or even the wind whistling through the labyrinth of chasms that litter the landscape. It might be the despondent wails of a young soul still not at rest even after the passage of a century, desperately seeking to bring attention to a heinous crime that has gone unpunished and unrecorded.

Chapter 9
Byng Inlet

Location: Byng Inlet lies north of Parry Sound. Turn west from Highway 69 onto Highway 529. After a few kilometres, turn onto Highway 645. This will take you to the shores of Georgian Bay and Byng Inlet.
Driving Time from Toronto: 3.5 hours.

More than a century and a half after lumbering began at Byng Inlet, logs are still being sawed into lumber at this isolated spot along the Georgian Bay shore. The operation today pales in comparison to what went before — in fact, it is little more than a cottage industry for Rolfe Burger — yet it keeps alive the memory of a day when the clamour of heavy industry filled the air and the sweet scent of freshly cut wood was inescapable.

Mr. Burger feels an intimate connection to the massive operation of yesteryear, since the logs he expertly crafts into furniture were actually cut 100 years earlier. They've lain dormant at the bottom of the bay, perfectly preserved by the minerals in the water since Byng Inlet's heyday as one of the largest and most prosperous milltowns anywhere in Canada. The hardworking lumbermen of long ago, men who toiled tirelessly to keep the sawmills here from slowing down, would surely smile down upon Mr. Burger's work, appreciating the fact that their labours and sacrifices are still bearing fruit.

Byng Inlet was conceived on the promise of wealth. During the summer of 1868, surveyor Vernon B. Wadsworth was dispatched by the Michigan-based Clarke, White and Company to locate appropriate sites at which to build mills that were to serve its newly acquired Magnetewan River timber limits. Wadsworth selected two spots on or near islets at the mouth of Byng Inlet. Here, the mills would be easily accessible by steamers operating on Georgian Bay in a sheltered cove where logs could be collected after being driven down from the interior highlands.

Two years later, Wadsworth returned again to survey another mill location, this time for the Dodge Lumber Company, which also had timber rights along the Magnetewan headwaters. On the instructions of his employers, he also laid out a village site adjacent to this third mill, naming it after the inlet upon which it was located. Little could he have known that this would become one of Canada's largest sawmill towns.

In its earliest days, Byng Inlet was little more than a rough-and-tumble frontier camp, where millhands and their families existed in a sprawl of ramshackle cabins without

*Byng Inlet was once among the largest and most
cosmopolitan towns on Georgian Bay. It boasted a theatre,
more than a dozen stores, coach service to the railway line,
and the fine hotel pictured here.*

sanitation or the niceties of civilization, often knee-deep in
either snow or the detritus of milling operations. It was hardly an Eden, and yet a vast fortune in lumber passed through
on its way to markets along the American east coast and in
the Midwest.

Sometime during the early 1870s, the Dodge Company
purchased the holdings of its rival, Clarke, White and Company.
The demand for lumber was so great that one of the newly
acquired mills was kept in operation to supplement Dodge's

own facility. By 1889, the firm employed 160 employees at the two mills with a production of 20 million board feet per year.

Later that year a forest fire destroyed the last Clarke White mill and the entire operation began to unravel. With trouble brewing elsewhere in its business empire, the Dodge Company began to divest itself of many of its farflung holdings. The Magnetewan timber rights and mills were sold to Merrill and Ring, a lumber conglomerate based out of Saginaw, Michigan.

If the residents of Byng Inlet thought Merrill and Ring was riding to their rescue, breathing new life into a moribund community, their hopes were soon dashed. The firm had no interest in the wellbeing of an isolated Canadian village and its people; they had milltowns of their own back in Michigan to worry about. Merrill and Ring continued to harvest the trees from the interior as before, but whereas previous firms had sawed the logs locally, the new owners opted to raft the logs across Lake Huron. This decision rescued several American communities that gone on life support when domestic sources of timber had been exhausted, but it put hundreds of men out of work in Byng Inlet. Predictably, the community went into a period of deep decline and most residents moved away in search of employment.

Ironically, Byng Inlet's salvation came courtesy of another Michigan-based lumber firm, Holland and Emery. In 1898, the Canadian government placed an embargo on the export of raw logs. Merrill and Ring, caught unprepared by the move, suddenly found themselves cut off from their timber supply. Disgusted, the company sold its Ontario holding to Holland and Emery, then operating near Bay City, Michigan. Holland and Emery closed its mill, moved it piece by piece across Lake Huron, and reassembled it at Byng Inlet.

During the course of its existence the operation existed under several guises, evolving from Holland and Emery to Holland and Graves, and ultimately to Holland, Bigwood and Company. One feature remained consistent throughout the years: it was among the largest lumber operations in Ontario, employing hundreds of men and turning out 200,000 board feet daily in two 10-hour shifts.

The facility consisted of two sawmills, box and lathe factories and a planing mill. Cut lumber was towed away by horse-drawn wagons along an extensive network of tramways and then stacked to dry for a year over an area that extended more than a mile inland. All summer long, an endless parade of steamers and schooners arrived in Byng Inlet to carry lumber to ports all over the Great Lakes.

Millhands lived in company-owned homes and boarding houses, and shopped at a company store. Direct current electricity for domestic lighting, a luxury then only available for the richest of individuals elsewhere, was directed into every home by generators located in the mill. Over time the town matured, as merchants and other professional men took up residence, establishing businesses and hammering out the first vestiges of a real community.

Within a few years, the community boasted a hotel, the company store, a two-room school, a church, a bakehouse, a blacksmith, an expansive series of wharves and a population of more than 600.

Despite its size, Byng Inlet remained isolated from civilization. The only practical link to the outside world was by steamer, while such roads that existed to and from town were little more than foot tracks impassible by wagon. During the winter months, the frozen waters of Georgian Bay provided a more direct and less taxing alternative to the roads, and many people took advantage of it to visit Parry Sound. But it was a risky venture. More than one person perished when the cutter they rode in fell through the ice.

This state of isolation ended when the Parry Sound-Sudbury branch of the Canadian Pacific Railroad (CPR) passed near Byng Inlet in 1908. The station was several miles inland, but for the first time an all-weather and affordable link to the outside world was available. It was common for residents to ride into Parry Sound on the morning train to do some shopping, and then return home on the evening train. The railway also provided another means by which the mill could ship lumber, and the only means available year-round.

There's little doubt the railway had a major impact on Byng Inlet. It boosted the fortunes of the lumber company, helped forge bonds with neighbouring communities and spurred growth by making the community more attractive to both prospective settlers and businesses. Some estimates claim Byng Inlet's population swelled well beyond 1,000 shortly after the railway's arrival.

As the town grew, it became more metropolitan. Both a dance hall and a movie house were built to entertain the locals, a stagecoach began operating between Byng Inlet and the railway station and as many as five stores opened for business. The sense of enthusiasm in the air was nearly tangible. Everyone was certain Byng Inlet was on the cusp of something great.

But all was not rosy in this tireless community. Byng Inlet's prosperity came at a steep price in blood and broken bodies. Lumbering was a dangerous job and the sawmill a lethal workplace. The various ways in which a man could be killed or maimed were too numerous to count.

A 13-year old boy, Patrick McNeil, was sliced in two by the saw. James Riddle, an experienced lumberman, fell off the elevated tramway and dropped 20 feet into the Magnetewan River below. He struck his head on a floating log and drowned. Another man was crushed under a load of cut lumber. Profit depended upon productivity, so when a worker was killed or wounded the mill usually continued with no more interruption than was required to get the bloody remains untangled from the machinery and the gore cleaned up.

Frank Peachey, a long-time millhand for Graves-Bigwood, which bought out the Dodge Lumber Company in the earlier twentieth century, vividly remembered one such tragic incident. It was a routine day at the mill, and the men were performing routine tasks. There was a hidden danger lurking just out of sight, however. Embedded deep within the heart of a log just entering the broad saw (essentially a giant band saw) was a metal spike. When the saw blade hit the spike it snapped, and began flailing about like the tentacles of some metallic octopus. The machine's operator, too slow in reacting, was beheaded. Management closed the mill for only a few hours in the wake of the tragic accident, though it did run the saws at half speed because, as Peachey said, "they didn't want the men to panic."

Fire was another constant threat at any sawmill. Powered by wood-fired steam plants and surrounded by flammable lumber and mill waste, sawmills had a terrible habit of catching fire and were routinely razed by flames. Often times, the damage was so great that the owners simply could not justify the cost of rebuilding, as was the case when the Dodge holdings were devastated in 1889.

Graves-Bigwood operated for some 14 seasons before fire reared its ugly head at Byng Inlet, but when at last the mill's good fortune had run its course the result was apocryphal. On May 20, 1912 a stray spark from the steam plant started a fire that was soon raging out of control. Flames began licking hungrily at the building's wooden structure and racing along floors, walls and ceilings. Workers fought a desperate battle against the firestorm, but in the end they were overwhelmed by the fury of the inferno.

When at last the smoke cleared to allow the citizens of

Byng Inlet to witness the extent of the damage, they were shocked to see only a charred scar where one of Canada's largest and most modern sawmills had stood only hours before. The destruction was complete. The mill itself was reduced to smouldering cinders, but more importantly the machinery was destroyed as well. In fact, the fire had burned so hot that some of the machinery had melted into unrecognizable slag. In addition, several nearby buildings and a great supply of lumber had been razed.

For the second time in its existence, Byng Inlet faced an uncertain future. Would Graves-Bigwood rebuild? The livelihood of hundreds depended on it. In the end, the community was lucky. The company had yet to exhaust its timber limits along the Magnetewan watershed, so rebuild it would. Bigger than ever, in fact. Within two years, a new mill was up and running. Business had returned to normal.

But this was only a short-term reprieve. Graves-Bigwood was felling trees at such a rate that only a decade later it began to feel the pinch as the supply diminished. Yet, they refused to alter their practices or slow down production. Graves-Bigwood cared nothing for the future of Byng Inlet; it was in business to maintain profits, not towns. In the cold-hearted reality of the lumber industry, Byng Inlet was a resource that, when its usefulness had expired, would be cast aside.

That day came in 1925 when the mill closed and Graves-Bigwood went in search of new stands of timber to exploit. Almost everyone followed, abandoning homes that no longer held any value or dreams. Byng Inlet disappeared virtually overnight, with but a small handful of stalwarts remaining behind to keep alive the community's memory. It was the same sad, yet entirely predictable, end as suffered by dozens of other lumber towns across the province.

While Byng Inlet may not be entirely dead, there is a melancholy, almost deathly silence about the faded town that has a wake-like quality. Mere shadows of long-ago glory are all that remain of the community today. And yet, visitors will find much to keep both cameras and imaginations busy.

Sawmill Lodge, a fishing resort operated by Rolfe Burger, occupies the site where the hotel once stood. The main building actually dates back to the 1920s and was formerly a general store. Today, it is a licensed restaurant and a showroom for the furniture Burger crafts from timber that has slept for decades at the bottom of the bay. In addition to making kitchen cabinets, wardrobes and tables, this enterprising gentleman markets the lumber wholesale for use in hardwood flooring — a unique way to bring a piece of history into your home.

On the grounds of Sawmill Lodge are the impressive remains of the mill. Walking in and around the stone foundations, the full extent of the operation becomes apparent. Only a fraction of the concrete foundations are visible — the remainder extend a distance back into the forest and are obscured by overgrown bush — and yet it is easy to imagine the massiveness of the mill, as if it were standing right in front of you.

Byng Inlet

Lining the shores of Byng Inlet there are rows of wooden pilings that slowly disappear into the waters. These posts that now lean at crazy angles once supported an extensive network of wharves by which lumber was shipped to hungry markets.

Several original buildings still remain to provide a glimpse into the brief heyday of the community. These include the ever-proud school, which stands with authority atop a granite hill just as one enters town; the church, in use today as an artist's gallery but still adding a special sense of faith to the community; and the bakery, which brings to mind the aroma of fresh-baked goods. Scattered around, you'll still find the odd home that once housed the tireless millhands.

A small cemetery hides alongside Highway 645 just a few miles out of town. Covered in shrubs and weeds, it appears as though no care has been lavished upon this final resting place for the men and women who lived and died — often under tragic circumstances — at Byng Inlet. Many tombstones are faded and others have fallen or become obscured by foliage. Still others have no doubt succumbed to the ravages of time.

In many ways, the cemetery is a reflection of the town it once served, for Byng Inlet, once one of Canada's most important sawmill communities, has been forgotten and neglected as well.

Bibliography

Brown, Ron. *Ghost Towns of Ontario: A Field Guide.* Toronto: Polar Press, 1997.

Brown, Ron. *Ontario's Secret Landscapes.* Erin: Boston Mills Press, 1999.

Bull, Perkins. *From Boyne to Brampton.* Toronto: George McLeod Ltd., 1936.*

Cobalt Historical Society. *The Heritage Silver Trail.* Cobalt, Ontario: The Highway Bookshop, 2000.

Fancy, Peter. *Temiskaming Treasure Trails.* Cobalt, Ontario: The Highway Bookshop, 1993.

Floren, Russell and Andrea Gutsche. *Ghosts of the Bay: A Guide to the History of Georgian Bay.* Toronto: Lynx Images, 1998.

Gilham, Elizabeth McClure. *Early Settlements of King Township, Ontario.* King City: Municipality of the Township of King, 1984.

Jordan, Shirley, John Bradley, et al. *Meanderings and Memories: Christie Township.* Christie, Ontario: Christie Historical Society, 1994.

Macfie, John. *Lots More ... Parry Sound Stories.* Parry Sound: The Hay Press, 2005.

Macfie, John. *Tales from Another Time: Oral History of Early Times in Parry Sound District.* Parry Sound: The Hay Press, 2000. *

McDevitt, Francis Vincent and Mary Margaret Munnoch.

Bibliography

Adjala. Erin, Ontario: Boston Mills Press, 1993. *

Smith, Barbara. *Ontario Ghost Stories.* Edmonton: Lone Pine Publishing, 1998.

Weber, Eldon D. (ed.) *Pioneer Hamlets of York.* Markham, Ontario: The Pennsylvania German Folklore Society of Ontario, 1977. *

*Publications that are marked with an * are the sources for the quotes within this book.

Acknowledgements

The authors wish to acknowledge the following individuals for providing personal memories of the ghost towns featured in this book: David Bond, Jim and Carol Bradley, Orma Faris, Russell Somerville, and Jack Sword. We also gratefully appreciate the assistance of Jay Murrell, Robert Keenan, Ethel Prescott and Larry Matthews for helping guide us in the right direction. Many others graciously assisted us with the manuscript: Kathleen Fry, Curator of the King Township Museum, who searched out historical photos on our behalf; Shirley Jordan of the Christie Historical Society, who provided so much insight into the history and people of Swords; Rolfe Burger at Byng Inlet, who took us on a guided tour of the locale and entertained us with enough stories for two chapters; and Dan Larocque of the Cobalt Welcome Centre, whose enthusiasm and knowledge inspired us in ways we can't describe. Finally, but of no less importance, we extend our warmest appreciation and respect to those innumerable individuals in local historical societies who endeavor to preserve the past, often without the credit they justly deserve.

Andrew Hind adds: I would like to thank John Beischer of *Farm Review*, who published my first ghost town article six years ago; it was the initial step in a long road eventually leading to this book. And of course, I have to extend my

Acknowledgements

admiration and thanks to Maria, who has trudged through innumerable overgrown fields and mosquito-infested forests at my side, searching with endless stoicism and boundless enthusiasm for the tales these ghost towns had to tell.

Maria Da Silva adds: I would like to thank Andrew for accompanying me on a journey into the past. It was an exciting experience, and we always found something different, from artifacts as small as spikes from lumber chutes to ruined buildings and foundations. To think that all those years have passed, and yet we could still find pieces of history hidden behind overgrown shrubs and amidst fields of weeds. But it was the people we met who made the villages come alive again; even if the relics won't always stay in our minds, these people will always remain in our hearts.

About the Authors

Andrew Hind is a freelance writer who lives in Bradford, Ontario. His feature articles have appeared in magazines and newspapers across Canada, in the United States and in England. Andrew developed a passion for history early on, especially for unusual and obscure events and people that are typically overlooked or quickly forgotten. He hopes, through his writing, to bring these fascinating stories to light for a modern audience.

Maria da Silva, who frequently contributes articles to the *Muskoka Sun*, has always had a passion for history and ghost stories. Coming from Portugal, a country that is full of history and the unknown, she never dreamed that her future would lead her into writing about the forgotten and the unexplained. Maria's work, co-authored with Andrew Hind, has appeared in publications such as *Fate, Mystery Magazine* and *Muskoka Magazine*.

Andrew and Maria are the authors of *Strange Events of Ontario,* and they also contributed to *Holiday Misadventures,* both published by James Lorimer and Company. Together, they are researching their next book — *Strange Events of Niagara.*

Index

Index

W